Popular
potatoes

Published by Hyndman Publishing
325 Purchas Road
RD 2 Amberley 7482

ISBN: 1-877382-24-8

TEXT: © Simon & Alison Holst

DESIGN: Dileva Design Ltd.

PHOTOGRAPHY: Lindsay Keats (except page 29, 76, 80 and 81 Sal Criscillo) Additional potato images from vegetables.co.nz

FOOD STYLING: Simon & Alison Holst

Because ovens and slow cookers vary, you should take the cooking times suggested in our recipes as guides only. The first time you make a recipe, check it towards the end of the suggested time to see if it is cooking faster, or more slowly than expected.

Always follow the detailed instructions given by manufacturers of your appliances and equipment, rather than the more general instructions given in these recipes.

Before You Start Cooking!

In this book you will often find potatoes are referred to by size.

A small new potato weighs about 50g. Allow 2–3 per serving

A medium-sized potato weighs about 125–150g

A large potato e.g. for baking weighs 200–250g

We have suggested using different potato types (waxy or new, all purpose or floury) in these recipes – you may (of course) use different types, but be aware this may affect the end result. Look on pages 6–7 for more information on potato varieties.

In potato cookery, you seldom need to be precise about weights, but the sizes and weights above will give you an indication.

If you use a baking dish bigger than that specified, the contents may cook more quickly. In a smaller dish, cooking time will probably be a little longer.

When parsley is specified, use fresh parsley, otherwise use fresh herbs when they are specified, and dried herbs at other times.

When coconut cream is used in a recipe, use standard or low fat canned coconut cream. (Freeze leftovers in small containers for later use.)

We have used microwave ovens of 700–750 Watts. If your microwave is of higher wattage, it will require a shorter cooking time. Use our times as a guide only.

For best results use standard metric measuring cups and spoons when you use these recipes. 1 metric cup holds 250ml. 1 tablespoon holds 15ml. 1 teaspoon holds 5ml. All of our cup and spoon measures are level unless otherwise stated.

Large amounts of butter are given by weight. Butter packs usually have 50g or 100g markings on the pack. 1 Tbsp butter weighs 15g.

Abbreviations used:

cm	centimeter	g	grams
°C	Celsius	tsp	teaspoon
ml	millilitre	Tbsp	tablespoon

Acknowledgements

We would like to thank the following for their assistance:

Horticulture NZ

Crop and Food Research

Glenda Gourley

Dennis Greville

Alison's Pantry

Bennicks Poultry Farm

For more information about other Holst titles, visit
www.holst.co.nz or **www.hyndman.co.nz**

About This Book

Everybody loves potatoes! We hope that this book will show you just how versatile potatoes can be. It contains over one hundred tasty and interesting potato recipes and includes all our favourites!

We think that our recipes will prove to you that potatoes are not only great value for money, but that they can be cooked (and enjoyed!) successfully by anyone, from inexperienced young starter cooks to busy mothers and fathers, or by experienced gourmets!

While we've tried to give some interesting ideas from around the world, you will also find that most of our recipes require only relatively few ingredients, many which you are likely to have on hand.

You can buy potatoes all year round, in small bags or large sacks, or you can grow your own potatoes in your garden if you have the space and the inclination. (We can't think of anything nicer than new potatoes cooked with a mint sprig, a few minutes after they are dug!) Do take time to read the details about potato varieties and their characteristics on pages 6 and 7, so you will be able to choose the potatoes which are best for your purpose.

Potatoes are good for you too! Alison has always remembered an interesting fact provided by the New Zealand Potato Board, when she worked for them many years ago. The message was that, if necessary, you can survive on nothing but potatoes, as long as you sit in the sun while you eat them! She also remembers that the two biggest fund-raising demonstrations she ever did (both to over 850 people!), one just north of Auckland and the other in Invercargill, were based around a variety of obviously very popular potato dishes!

'Popular Potatoes' has new and recent recipes from Simon and Alison, lots of new photographs and includes most of the recipes in 'Alison Holst's Best Potato Recipes', which is now out of print, but sold over 100,000 copies.

We hope you will enjoy these recipes as much as we do!

Simon & Alison Holst

Handy tips and facts

Look out for me and other spuddies through this book – we've got handy tips and facts to share about potatoes.

CONTENTS

The Not So Humble Potato...

It seems it's quite easy to take the poor old potato more than a little for granted. However, if you're willing to take a little time to scratch (perhaps that should be dig in the case of potatoes!) below the surface a number of interesting facts come to light, and by taking the time to read a few basics, you may be able to enhance your enjoyment (and diet!).

It seems that potatoes are among the quiet achievers – did you know that they're the world's fourth largest food crop? Or that they are grown in more countries than any other crop except maize?

Closer to home the statistics also make interesting reading. New Zealand produces over 250,000 tonnes of fresh potatoes a year, and over 97% of the population eat them – this must put them in a fairly elite category of foods. In fact, 54% of New Zealanders eat potatoes four times a week, which might help account for the approximately 65kg we eat per person, per year (globally this puts us ahead of the US at 61kg/year but some way behind the UK at 105kg/year).

Potatoes and nutrition

As most people know, potatoes are an excellent source of carbohydrate (the body's preferred fuel source), and in their natural state are virtually fat free. But did you know that Kiwis actually get around 30% of their vitamin C from potatoes? Or that they are a valuable source of B group vitamins, particularly B6, thiamin and niacin and are a good source of fibre? As if that's not enough, they also contain some iron and magnesium. No wonder potatoes count towards your "5 plus a day" servings of fruit and vegetables!

Remember that while potatoes themselves are not fattening, some cooking and preparation methods are! Deep frying chips and/or roasting potatoes swimming in fat or oil will change them to a high fat food, which should be eaten in small quantities only!

Potatoes have so much flavour and nutrients in, or just under their skins, it's a pity to throw it away! (A microwaved or baked potato in its skin contains more fibre than two slices of wholemeal bread!) Instead of peeling them, try rubbing washed potatoes with "green scratchies" (otherwise known as rectangular green plastic scouring pads or pot scrubs). Not only is this quicker and easier than peeling, it removes the stubborn dirt, leaving most of the skin intact – and you finish up with more potato for your money.

Treated like this, you will find you can leave the skin on potatoes used for roasting, boiling, or in salads! (You can even mash potatoes with their skin on – then you can be trendy and call them "smashed" potatoes, but these aren't really quite the same as good old mash!)

If you MUST peel potatoes, use a sharp potato peeler in preference to a vegetable knife. A peeler removes a thinner layer than the knife does, saving money as well as nutrients. If you are going to peel them, do so just before you are going to cook them – if you leave them exposed to air some of the nutrients will oxidise (causing discolouration) and covering them in water to prevent this means some of the nutrients will be leeched out.

To retain maximum nutrients when boiling potatoes, keep the pieces large and don't use more water than you need. Always have a lid on the pot.

What to look for when buying potatoes

Try to choose potatoes that haven't got any cuts, bruises, green patches or shoots. Remember however, that although it's tempting to choose a smooth looking potato over a misshapen one, and assume that it is a better product, this is not necessarily the case. Some varieties have skins which are rougher and/or have more eyes in them. A potato does not have to look good to cook brilliantly!

For best results it more important to select the right potato for the job! The texture of a cooked potato varies with the variety, the time of the year (season) and the soil and climatic conditions it was grown in. Unless you are an expert, you are unlikely to be able to determine all of these factors just by looking at the potato. Thankfully, to make life easier, most bags of potatoes are labelled with both the variety, and how they are best used.

They may be marked as most suitable for 'boiling', 'salads', 'mashing', 'wedges' or 'baking', for example. This is largely determined by their cooked texture – in general a potato is either 'floury' (best for mashing, roasting or baking), or 'waxy' (great for eating boiled or in salads) or all purpose (somewhere in between floury and waxy, and generally suitable for most cooking methods).

Why are potatoes sometimes different?

Different varieties of potatoes do tend to fall into broad categories of waxy, floury or all purpose, however, to complicate things a little, this can also be affected by the time of the year (season) the potato is planted and harvested, the soil and the weather. For example, an Ilam Hardy harvested early in the season (October) is quite waxy. However if the potatoes are left to mature longer before harvesting the Ilam Hardy becomes a good general-purpose potato, whilst if left even longer, towards the end of the season when a lot more of the natural sugars have converted to starch, it tends to be floury. This is the difference between "New" or "Main crop" potatoes you will sometimes hear about. To further complicate the issue, not all potato varieties show such a range of characteristics.

Weather, climate and soil also have a dramatic effect on the cooking performance of a potato. For example, a Southland grown Nadine may be very waxy whilst a Pukekohe grown Nadine may be only slightly waxy. The flavour is also influenced.

How to store your potatoes

For best results, store potatoes in a well ventilated, cool, dark place. Don't put them in the fridge as the flavour changes will be noticeable (the starch will begin to convert into sugar). Always remove them from any plastic packaging (this helps prevent sweating), unless it is a 'Greenguard' bag, which is manufactured specifically for potatoes. A heavy paper bag or cardboard box makes a good storage container.

Remember, place them gently in your storage area – although they may seem tough, they bruise easily if you drop them or treat them roughly, so for best flavour and less waste, look after them.

When potatoes are exposed to light they can develop a green colour resulting in chlorophyll formation in the surface layers. Associated with this is the formation of a toxic alkaloid, solanine. The amount of green pigment depends on the intensity of the light, length of exposure and age of potato. New potatoes are really susceptible to greening. Some varieties have quite a yellow flesh so don't confuse this with greening. If you do purchase potatoes with lots of greening, return them to your retailer. If there are small amounts of greening simply peel or scrape away the greening and use the potato normally.

Natural dirt and dust on potatoes can help to keep them fresher so it is best not to wash them until you are ready to cook them – or if you buy ready washed, buy small quantities regularly.

Different types of potatoes

Waxy
most 'early' new season varieties

These potatoes tend to be waxy and are ideal for boiling, salads, casseroles, soups.

Draga

Waxy/floury

These potatoes tend to be general-purpose making them suitable for most end uses.

Rua

Floury

These potatoes tend to be floury and are ideal for mashing, wedges, chips, roasting, baking.

Ilam Hardy

Be sure to use a potato best suited to your cooking method.

Some potatoes are less floury or less waxy than others. These potatoes fall into the area of 'general-purpose' and will tend to perform more tasks, although perhaps with not as good results as the ones which clearly fall into the floury or waxy category.

Nadine

Frisia

And limited or localised supplies of Jersey Bennie, Liseta, Red King Edward, Tiffany.

Desiree

Karaka

Moonlight

And limited or localised supplies of Red Ruby, Rocket, Maris Anchor.

Red Rascal

Agria

Fianna

And limited or localised supplies of White Delight.

Souper
Potatoes

Potatoes make wonderful soups! When they are cooked then puréed in stock, they make a smooth and creamy soup, and when the cooked, cubed potatoes are left in small pieces throughout a soup or chowder, they have just the right texture – not too firm, and not too soft. Enjoy our soups, then try making your own specialties, adding different vegetables and seasonings!

Corn, Ham & Potato Chowder

A big bowl of this thick, creamy soup, packed with corn, other vegetables and ham, makes a satisfying meal on a cold day. By working efficiently and using a few short cuts, you can have it on the table in 20 minutes.

FOR 3–4 LARGE SERVINGS:

1 Tbsp oil
½–1 tsp minced or finely chopped garlic
1 large onion, peeled and halved
1 medium carrot, scrubbed
2 cups hot water
2 medium–large (about 300g) all purpose or floury
    potatoes, scrubbed
1 leek or 2 tender celery stalks, optional
2–3 tsp instant chicken or bacon stock powder
50g butter
¼ cup flour
2 cups milk
2 tsp basil pesto, optional
1 x 440g can cream-style corn
100–200g chunky ham pieces
chopped parsley and chives

In a large pot over moderate heat, heat the oil and garlic while you chop the onion into 7mm cubes. Stir the prepared onion into the oil and keep cooking the mixture while you chop the carrot into 5mm cubes. Add the hot water, then the prepared carrot. While the mixture simmers, cut the potatoes into 7mm cubes and thinly slice the celery or leek if using. Add the vegetables and the stock powder to the pot, cover and leave the vegetables to finish cooking while you make the sauce.

Melt the butter in a medium–large pot. Stir in the flour and heat until it bubbles, without letting it brown. Add the milk, half a cup at a time, stirring constantly and bringing to the boil before the next addition. When it boils after the last measure of milk is added, remove the pot from the heat and stir in the pesto, if using, and the corn.

Finely chop the ham chunks, then as soon as the potato and carrot are tender, tip the sauce and the ham and parsley into the large pot with the vegetables. Stir to mix thoroughly, and cook for a few minutes to heat through, without actually letting the mixture boil. Serve in large bowls with warmed crusty bread or rolls.

VARIATIONS: To make Corn and Bacon Chowder, leave out the ham, but brown 2–4 chopped bacon rashers in the oil before adding the garlic and chopped onion. To save time, replace the onion, carrot and celery with 4 cups frozen vegetables.

Leek & Potato Soup

This is a delicately flavoured, smooth, creamy and filling winter soup that uses inexpensive winter vegetables. While our version is not traditional, it is quick and easy to make without the bother of white sauce. The amount of cream you use is up to your taste and your conscience!

FOR 4–6 SERVINGS:

50g butter
1 clove garlic, crushed
3 medium leeks, white and pale green parts only, finely
    sliced
3 medium (400–450g) all purpose or floury potatoes
4 cups water
3 tsp instant chicken stock
1 tsp instant green herb stock
1 tsp sugar
about ¼ cup cream
salt, pepper and hot sauce to taste
extra cream and chopped chives or ground paprika to
    garnish, optional

Melt the butter in a large pot. Chop the garlic and add the leeks. Cover and gently cook for about 10 minutes. Take care not to let the vegetables brown at all during this stage.

Peel and thinly slice the potatoes, then chop the slices into quarters. Add to the pot along with the water, both stock powders and the sugar. Simmer for about 10 minutes until both the leeks and potatoes are just tender. (Overcooking will spoil the fresh flavour of the vegetables.)

Blend or process the vegetable mixture until smooth and creamy or, if you want a chunky soup, mash with a potato masher. Return to the pot and stir in the cream, then taste before adding the seasonings.

Reheat gently and serve immediately or reheat when required. Swirl a little runny cream on top of each bowl of soup, or top each bowl with a spoonful of lightly whipped cream. Sprinkle with chopped chives or paprika if desired.

NOTE: Sometimes leeks come with dirt between their layers of leaves. If you cut each leek in half lengthwise, then hold it under a running tap cut side up, you should be able to get rid of most of the soil before you chop them crosswise.

Chunky Shrimp & Potato Chowder

This delicious, chunky chowder is one of Alison's favourite soups. Keep a can of shrimps in your store cupboard so you can make it at short notice as a satisfying meal for unexpected guests. You can also double the quantities of everything – as long as you have a large enough pot!

FOR 4–6 SERVINGS:

25g butter
2 medium onions, chopped
1 cup sliced celery, optional
1 cup hot water
1 tsp instant green herb stock powder
1 tsp instant chicken stock powder
3 medium (450g) all purpose or floury potatoes, scrubbed
    and cut into 1cm cubes
about 1 cup frozen mixed vegetables or peas
1 x 200g can shrimps
2 cups milk
about 2 Tbsp cornflour
chopped parsley and a pinch of paprika to garnish

Gently heat the butter in a large pot. Add the onions – and celery if using – and cook, covered, until tender but not browned. Add the water, stock powders, and the potatoes.

Cover and simmer for 15 minutes or until the potatoes are tender, adding the frozen vegetables three-quarters of the way through so they will be cooked at the same time as the potatoes.

Add the shrimps and the liquid from the can (unless it is dark in colour and very strongly flavoured) and the milk. Bring the mixture to the boil. Thicken with the cornflour which has been mixed with a little water to form a paste. Taste and adjust the seasonings as required.

Serve in large bowls for lunch or dinner, garnished with parsley and paprika, with toast or bread rolls alongside.

VARIATIONS:

Add a spoonful of lightly whipped cream for special occasions.

For Chunky Salmon & Potato Chowder, replace the shrimps with canned salmon. Break the salmon into smallish chunks, removing and discarding the bones and any dark skin. Use all the salmon liquid in the chowder.

Potato, Garlic & Thyme Soup

This simple soup, made from basic ingredients, is particularly delicious if made with good stock. Always season the soup carefully before serving it. Home-grown thyme from your garden has a stronger flavour than very young thyme plants, so you will need to use larger quantities if you use the young, hothouse variety. Add smaller amounts of dried thyme instead, if you like.

FOR 4 SERVINGS:

1 large onion
3 large cloves garlic
1 Tbsp butter
1 Tbsp canola or olive oil
500g floury potatoes
1 Tbsp fresh thyme leaves, chopped
3 cups chicken or vegetable stock
seasoning to taste
¼ cup cream or Greek-style yoghurt, plus extra to
    garnish
fresh thyme leaves and ground paprika to garnish

Peel and halve the onion, then chop finely. Cut off the root ends of the garlic cloves, bang them with the bottom of a bottle to loosen the skins, then chop finely. Put the prepared onion and garlic in a medium pot with the butter and oil and cook over low to moderate heat, covered, until the onion is clear but not browned.

Meantime, thinly peel the potatoes, then chop into 1cm cubes. Add to the pot with the thyme, then stir in the chicken or vegetable stock (or use the same volume of water plus 4 teaspoons instant chicken or vegetable stock). Simmer for 15 minutes until the potatoes are tender.

Purée the mixture in a food processor, mouli fitted with a fine blade or a wand. Taste and season if necessary, then stir in the cream.

Just before serving, reheat, but do not boil. Serve in bowls, topped with a swirl of cream or Greek yoghurt, a few thyme leaves, and a sprinkling of paprika.

NOTE: Greek yoghurt has a less tangy flavour than plain yoghurt, which can overwhelm the other flavours in this soup.

 Don't feel you should always peel potatoes – rub off any rough bits using a "green scratchy", and eat the skins too – the skins are particularly tasty and fibre-rich!

Fish Chowder

Fish chowder makes an excellent meal at any time of the year. This version is light enough to serve during summer, but is also warm and comforting on a cold winter's evening.

FOR 3–4 SERVINGS:

1 Tbsp olive oil
25g butter
1 medium onion, diced
100g bacon, diced
2 sticks celery, thinly sliced
2 medium (300g) all purpose or floury potatoes, cut into 1cm cubes
1 medium carrot, finely diced
2½ cups milk
½ tsp garlic salt
500g fish fillets, cubed
1 Tbsp chopped fresh dill, optional
1 Tbsp cornflour
salt and pepper to taste
chopped fresh dill or parsley to garnish

Heat the oil and butter together in a large pot. Add the onion and cook until the onion softens. Add the bacon, celery, potato and carrot to the pot and cook, stirring frequently to prevent browning, for about 5 minutes.

Add 2 cups of the milk and the garlic salt and simmer for about 10 minutes or until the potato is just tender, then add the cubed fish – and dill if using. Mix the remaining milk with the cornflour to form a paste and add to the pot. Bring the chowder to the boil, then reduce the heat and simmer for 5 minutes.

Season to taste, then ladle into large bowls, garnish with chopped herbs and serve accompanied with crusty garlic bread.

NOTE: To make easy garlic bread for 4, mix 2 tablespoons of olive oil or melted butter with a finely chopped clove of fresh garlic. Lightly brush both sides of 4 thick, diagonally sliced lengths of French bread with the garlic mixture. Grill, turning once, until both sides are golden brown (watch closely to prevent burning).

Cool Potato
Salads

Using new potatoes or waxy potato varieties, you can make really interesting salads right through the year! Potato salads are substantial enough to be served as the main part of lunch, and are also excellent served in warm weather with barbecues, steaks or cold meat, as the main meal of the day. Potato salads travel well in packed lunches too, and they are a real boon for family cooks who like a salad that can be made ahead, then refrigerated.

Salad Niçoise

This salad makes a wonderful hot weather lunch or a light evening meal course. It always looks best if you arrange the ingredients, one at a time, on individual dinner plates.

FOR 2 SERVINGS:

2 large eggs
4–6 small new or waxy potatoes
100–150g green beans
mixed lettuce leaves, including small cos lettuce leaves
2 medium or 8–10 baby tomatoes
10cm telegraph cucumber
1 x 185–200g can tuna
2–4 spring onions, diagonally sliced
4–6 anchovy fillets, whole or chopped
8–12 black olives, whole or sliced

DRESSING:

2 Tbsp lemon juice
6 Tbsp olive oil
1 tsp Dijon mustard
¼ tsp salt

Hard-boil the eggs and cook the potatoes and beans until just tender at least 30 minutes before serving time. Cool the potatoes and beans in cold water, then drain and set aside.

While the vegetables are cooking, chop the remaining ingredients as required.

Just before you are ready to serve, arrange the lettuce leaves on two dinner plates so that the tips are close to the edge of the plates and the stems are towards the centre. Thickly slice the potatoes and beans if required and peel and quarter the eggs. Slice the tomatoes if using medium ones. Cut the cucumber in half lengthwise, scoop out the seeds with a teaspoon, then cut in crosswise slices.

Arrange the prepared salad vegetables on the lettuce. Drain and flake the tuna, and spoon over the salad. Top with the spring onion, anchovies and olives.

Just before serving, combine the dressing ingredients in a screw-topped jar and drizzle over the plates. Serve with French or garlic bread.

NOTE: Vary the quantities of any of the ingredients to suit yourself.

Sausage & Potato Salad with Mustard Dressing

New potatoes and sliced precooked sausages taste really good when you mix them with this dressing! Make the salad with your favourite precooked specialty deli sausages, with frankfurters, or even leftover fried or barbecued sausages. You will end up with more dressing than you need, but you can refrigerate it for later use.

FOR 4 SERVINGS:

about 300g new or waxy potatoes

DRESSING:

¼ cup wholegrain mustard
2 Tbsp brown sugar
2 Tbsp wine vinegar
1 large clove garlic, roughly chopped
1 Tbsp roughly chopped parsley
1 Tbsp roughly chopped chives or spring onions
1 Tbsp chopped fresh coriander, optional
½ cup olive or canola oil
¼ cup warm water

200–300g cooked sausages
4–6 gherkins, optional
2–4 pickled onions, optional
about 2 cups coarsely chopped crisp lettuce

Scrape the potatoes, cutting them in half if they are large and place in a pot with just enough lightly salted water to cover and simmer for about 20 minutes or until they are tender (test with a sharp knife). Remove the pot from the heat and leave the potatoes to stand in the water for 5 minutes.

Make the dressing next. Measure the first three ingredients into the bowl of a food processor or into a blender. Add the garlic, parsley and chives. With the motor running, slowly add the oil, followed by the water. Taste and add extra sugar if required. The consistency of the finished dressing should be between that of mayonnaise and French dressing.

Drain and slice the warm potatoes, then gently toss them in enough dressing to coat. Cut the sausages into slices about 5mm thick and separately toss them in enough dressing to coat. Leave to stand for a few minutes so the dressing will flavour the sausages.

Gently mix together the prepared sausages and potatoes. Finely slice or chop the gherkins and pickled onions if using, and add to the salad.

Serve the salad on a bed of chopped lettuce on individual plates or shallow bowls.

NOTE: If the wholegrain mustard you use is sweet, start with half the amount of brown sugar.

For extra colour, add some tomato wedges to the salad just before serving.

Use the dressing immediately or refrigerate in a covered container, but bring to room temperature before using.

American Potato Salad

This is a wonderful salad if you make it with good mayonnaise. Make it the day you are going to serve it and refrigerate it promptly.

FOR 2–3 SERVINGS:

2 cups cooked, cubed new or waxy potatoes
1 Tbsp wine vinegar
1 Tbsp olive oil
1 spring onion, finely chopped
2 Tbsp chopped parsley
¼ cup traditional mayonnaise or Best Foods Mayonnaise
½–1 large hard-boiled egg, peeled and chopped
extra chopped parsley

Put the cubed potatoes in a plastic bag, then add the vinegar and the oil. Mix gently, without breaking up the potatoes.

Mix together in a shallow bowl the next three ingredients, then add the potato mixture and the egg and fold through.

Just before serving, sprinkle with a little extra parsley.

Cover and refrigerate until ready to serve.

Traditional Mayonnaise

Home-made mayonnaise is just as good as, if not better than, the best quality bought mayonnaise, and costs a fraction of the price.

FOR ABOUT 2 CUPS:

2 large eggs
½ cup white wine vinegar
1 tsp salt
1 tsp sugar
1–2 tsp mixed mustard
1–2 garlic cloves, crushed, optional
fresh or dried herbs to taste, optional
1½–2 cups canola oil

Put the metal chopping blade in the food processor. Add the first five ingredients. Process to mix. With the machine on, add the oil in a thin stream through the tube in the lid.

The mixture will keep getting thicker as more oil is added, so stop adding oil as soon as the mayonnaise is the thickness you like it to be.

If you are adding the optional ingredients, add them after you have added a cup of the oil.

If you have added the optional ingredients, it is best to leave the mayonnaise to stand for a while until the flavours intensify, before using any of it. Cover and refrigerate in a jar for up to 3 weeks. (Don't leave your jar of homemade mayonnaise standing round in a warm kitchen – always keep it in the refrigerator.)

NOTES: You can also make this mayonnaise in a blender or small food processor. If you do this, halve the quantities.

Don't leave out the mustard as it helps the mayonnaise become thick and smooth.

Cumin Potato Salad

It is surprisingly quick and easy to make interesting salad dressings yourself from scratch. Try this zingy dressing to add zest to a salad made from lovely, waxy new potatoes – be sure to use freshly ground cumin.

MAKES ABOUT 1 CUP:

1 Tbsp onion pulp (see below)
½ cup olive oil
½ cup white wine vinegar
2 tsp ground cumin
¾ tsp salt
1–2 tsp crumbled dried oregano leaves
1 clove garlic
freshly ground black pepper to taste
hot pepper sauce to taste

To make the onion pulp, cut an onion in half horizontally, then scrape the cut surface with a sharp-edged teaspoon. (The other half of the onion can be refrigerated and used later.)

Combine all the ingredients in a clean, dry screw-top jar.

Pour as much of the dressing as you like over warm, chopped or cubed cooked new or waxy potato slices and mix gently until they are coated with the dressing. If desired, add some lightly cooked chopped green beans to the dressed potatoes, then toss gently again.

Sprinkle the salad with finely chopped parsley, coriander, and spring onions or chives. Cover and leave to stand at room temperature for about 30 minutes before serving with a tomato salad and barbecued meat, sliced ham, or cold roast meat.

Hot-Smoked Salmon with Potato Salad

Celebrate the arrival of summer with this delicious, warm salad. The combination of smoked salmon and new potatoes works particularly well and makes for a surprisingly substantial salad.

You can smoke your own salmon (see below), but a 200g pack of commercially hot-smoked salmon is just as good.

FOR 2 SERVINGS:

2 slices, each about 150g, fresh skinless salmon
1 Tbsp brown sugar
1 tsp salt

250g–300g new or waxy potatoes
about 150g small green beans
¼ cup olive oil
2 Tbsp lemon juice
1 Tbsp Dijon or other mustard
2 Tbsp capers
2 spring onions, sliced
salt, pepper and sugar to taste
¼ cup mayonnaise
1 Tbsp each lemon juice and warm water
1 tsp finely grated lemon rind
salad greens

To smoke the salmon, place it (skin-side down) on a sheet of doubled tin foil with the corners twisted to hold in the juices. Thoroughly mix the sugar and salt and sprinkle it over the salmon. Place the salmon, still in the foil, in the smoker and follow the manufacturer's instructions. We fuel ours with ¼–½ cup methylated spirits, and use 1 cup manuka chips dampened with ¼ cup of water. Smoke for about 15–20 minutes.

Halve the potatoes if large, then simmer in lightly salted water until tender, adding the whole beans in the last 5 minutes. Drain the vegetables and immediately cool the beans under cold water, then cool, skin and slice the potatoes. Set aside while you make the dressing and finish the mayonnaise.

Combine the oil and the next four ingredients in a screw-top jar. Shake to mix, then season to taste. In a separate container combine the mayonnaise with the lemon juice and warm water, then stir in the lemon rind.

Gently mix the sliced potatoes and beans in the mustard dressing. Arrange the salad greens on two plates. Top with the dressed potatoes and beans, finishing with some salmon. Drizzle with lemon mayonnaise and serve immediately.

Hot Potato Salad

If you like the idea of warm food with a tangy sauce or dressing, try this recipe which is perfect for cooler late spring or early summer days when the idea of a salad is appealing, but it is not quite warm enough for a cold meal. Because freshly dug new potatoes are among our favourite foods, we often cook more than we need – leftovers are delicious served like this!

FOR 2–3 SERVINGS:

2–3 bacon rashers
1 onion, finely chopped
2 tsp flour
about 1 tsp sugar
about ½ tsp each salt and dry mustard
about ½ cup water
2–3 Tbsp white wine vinegar
4 medium cooked new or waxy potatoes
2 gherkins or dill pickles
chopped parsley to garnish
pinch of paprika, optional

Cook the bacon in a medium frypan until crisp, then remove it from the pan and let it cool on a folded paper towel.

Add the onion to the bacon drippings in the pan and cook, covered, until the onion is transparent and straw-coloured.

Stir the flour, sugar, salt and mustard into the onion in the pan, then add the water and bring to the boil, stirring constantly, until the sauce thickens. Add 2 tablespoons of the vinegar and stir over low heat until the dressing comes back to the boil. Taste and add the extra vinegar if you like a more tangy dressing, and more water if the sauce has thickened too much to coat the potatoes thinly. Adjust the seasonings as required – the strongly flavoured sauce should taste both sweet and sour.

Slice the cooked potatoes and the gherkins into the dressing. Set aside, covered, until ready to serve.

Just before serving reheat the mixture, stirring occasionally, taking care not to break up the potato pieces.

Serve in a shallow bowl, sprinkled with the chopped bacon, chopped parsley, and a sprinkling of paprika if desired.

Serve with hot frankfurters or sausages, or cold meat such as corned beef, roast lamb or pork.

Potato salads are always popular! Vary them, trying thin dressings as well as creamy ones. For best flavour, add the dressing ahead of time to allow the flavours in the dressing to be absorbed by the potatoes.

Peanutty Potato Salad

This high-protein peanutty dressing is an Indonesian specialty, known as 'gado gado'.

It turns cold, cooked potatoes – and other vegetables – into a very satisfying meal.

DRESSING:

2 tsp canola or other oil
1 onion, finely chopped
1 large garlic clove, finely chopped
2 tsp brown sugar
2 tsp Kikkoman soy sauce
2 tsp lemon juice
¼ cup of crunchy or smooth peanut butter
water or coconut cream
hot pepper sauce to taste

cooked waxy or new potatoes, quartered or sliced
cooked beans, chopped into 5cm lengths
cucumber, peeled and thickly sliced
spring onions, chopped
hard-boiled eggs, peeled and quartered
tofu, cubed and fried
beansprouts
crisp lettuce leaves

Heat the oil in a frypan and cook the onion and garlic until tender. Stir in the brown sugar, soy sauce, lemon juice and peanut butter. Stir over low heat, then add enough water and/or coconut cream to thin the sauce to pouring consistency. Add enough pepper sauce to taste. Pour the sauce into a jug and set aside.

Arrange the first seven ingredients for the salad accompaniments in bowls on the table with the jug of peanutty sauce. Place 1–2 lettuce leaves on individual plates, then encourage diners to help themselves to the accompaniments, finishing up with some sauce poured over the salad.

Spicy Yoghurt Potato Salad Dressing

We are great believers in cooking more potatoes than we need for a meal because having a ziplock bag of cooked potatoes in the refrigerator is like having money in the bank – always useful!

In warm weather we use cold, cooked new potatoes to make this low-calorie creamy salad with its spicy flavour, and serve it with barbecued butterflied lamb, lamb kebabs, steak or interesting sausages. During colder weather we make it from leftover, firm-textured main crop potatoes – it is marvellous as a side dish for curries.

MAKES ABOUT 1 CUP:

1 large clove garlic, peeled
½–1 small green chilli, deseeded and roughly chopped
¼ cup fresh coriander leaves, roughly chopped
2 spring onions, roughly chopped
1 tsp ground cumin
½ tsp sugar
½ tsp salt
1 cup plain unsweetened yoghurt

Combine the first seven ingredients in a food processor, then process until finely chopped. Add the yoghurt and pulse just enough to combine.

Gently mix the dressing through leftover cubed potatoes using proportions to suit yourself.

To retain nutrients when boiling potatoes, keep the pieces large and don't use more water than you need. Always have a lid on the pot.

If you have one, use a steamer above another pot to cook potatoes. Steaming retains nutrients which are otherwise lost.

Snacking
on Spuds

The following recipes are a really mixed bunch! Some make tasty finger food, others are very

good for breakfasts, while some will especially please those who like interesting spicy dishes.

Potato Pancakes

A cross between hash browns and fritters, these are especially popular with children who enjoy their crisp texture and mild flavour. The bacon adds interest, but you can leave it out, especially if you are serving the pancakes with meat and a salad.

FOR 6–8 SERVINGS (16 PANCAKES):

2 large eggs, unbeaten
2 Tbsp milk
2 rashers lean bacon or ham, very finely chopped
1 onion, very finely chopped
1 tsp curry powder
1 tsp celery salt
3–4 medium (about 500g) all purpose or floury potatoes, scrubbed or peeled
¼ cup flour
vegetable oil for frying

Mix together the eggs, milk, bacon, onion and seasonings in a large bowl.

Just before cooking, grate the potatoes into the mixture, then add the flour.

Put just enough oil in a frypan to cover the bottom. Heat until a small test amount of the pancake mixture bubbles when put in. Drop in dessertspoonsful of the mixture, four at a time, using a second spoon to stop the mixture from sticking to the first spoon. Try to make even-shaped pancakes, flattening them a little if necessary. Cook each pancake for 3–4 minutes per side, until golden brown and cooked through to the centre. As they are cooked, transfer the pancakes to a paper towel on a flat plate and place in a warm oven.

Serve alone, or with tomatoes and/or mushrooms etc. for a light meal. Or, serve as finger food, topped with sour cream and a little smoked salmon (or other topping/s).

VARIATION: Omit the bacon or ham and serve the pancakes with chops, steak, sausages and cooked vegetables or your favourite salad for dinner.

Pea Flour Patties

In this eggless recipe, small pieces of raw vegetables are incorporated into an Indian spice-flavoured batter. Try them served hot alongside a yoghurt-based dip.

FOR 4 SERVINGS:

1 cup pea flour
about ½ cup water
1 tsp turmeric
2 tsp ground cumin
2 tsp ground coriander seed
2 tsp garam masala
2 medium (about 300g) waxy or all purpose potatoes
1 onion
1 cup frozen peas or other vegetables
oil for frying

Mix the pea flour with the water and the next four ingredients to make a fairly stiff paste. Leave to stand for 5 minutes or longer, while you prepare the vegetables.

Scrub the potatoes using a 'green scratchy' (see page 4). Cut the potatoes and the other vegetables into pea-sized cubes.

Mix the vegetables into the batter just before you intend to start making the patties; you may need to thicken the batter by adding extra pea flour to make it thick enough to keep the vegetables together.

Pour the oil into a frypan to a depth of 2cm. Heat, then drop in teaspoonfuls of mixture, a few at a time. Adjust the heat so the patties cook and brown nicely in about 4 minutes, then turn and cook the other side for the same time. Faster cooking will result in raw vegetables inside the batter. As the patties are cooked, transfer them to a shallow plate covered with absorbent paper napkins. Alternatively serve them as finger food with your favourite toppings.

Serve immediately as finger food, with a herby dip made by combining plain unsweetened yoghurt, lemon juice, chopped mint, salt and a little sugar to suit your taste.

Did you know that 54% of Kiwis eat potatoes four times a week?

For an easy lunch at work, take a potato to microwave, and a small can of flavoured tuna. How easy is that!

Filo Samosas

Everyone enjoys the interesting contrast of a light flaky crust with the dense, well-seasoned potato filling of these little pastries. Although they are a simplified version of a traditional Indian vegetarian snack, they still contain quite a few ingredients. Use as many as possible, but if you have to leave out a few seasonings, we are sure you will still enjoy them.

FOR 8 SMALL SAMOSAS (4 SERVINGS):

2 medium (about 300g) all purpose or floury potatoes
1 Tbsp oil
1 medium onion, finely chopped
1½ tsp curry powder
1 tsp ground cumin
½ tsp garam masala
½ tsp ground coriander seeds
¾ cup frozen peas
2 Tbsp water
1 tsp salt
½ tsp sugar
juice of ½ lemon
2 Tbsp chopped mint or fresh coriander leaves
6 sheets filo pastry
25g butter, melted

Scrub and cut the potatoes into 1cm cubes. Cook in a lidded microwave container (see page 4) or in a pot in a little water until tender.

Heat the oil in a large frypan. Gently cook the onion and all the seasonings until the onion is tender. Add the peas and the water, cover and cook for 2 minutes. Add the drained, cooked potatoes, salt, sugar and lemon juice, and mix thoroughly, without breaking up the potato too much. Taste and add extra salt and lemon juice if required. Stir in the chopped herbs.

Preheat the oven to 200°C.

Stack together three lightly buttered sheets of filo. Cut crosswise into four even strips. Put a good tablespoon of filling at the end of one strip and fold into a triangular parcel (see diagram below).

Repeat this step with the remaining filo sheets and filling mixture. Lightly brush the top of each samosa with melted butter. Place on a baking tray.

Bake the samosas for 10 minutes then reduce the heat to 180°C and bake for a further 15–20 minutes until golden brown.

Serve warm, as a snack or a light meal, at any time of the day.

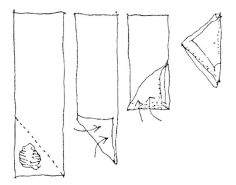

Jacket Wedges

These jacket wedges make great snacks that are popular with all age groups. Keep wedges interesting by experimenting and adding different spices and flavourings to the coating mixture so they are never exactly the same twice. Serve straight from the oven, in a shallow basket or bowl lined with paper towels, or serve them on a large platter, surrounding one or more bought or homemade dips – the sky's the limit!

FOR 3–4 SERVINGS:

4 large (1kg) all purpose or floury potatoes
3 Tbsp olive or canola oil
1 Tbsp light soya sauce
1 tsp very finely chopped garlic
1 Tbsp finely grated parmesan cheese
½ tsp salt

Preheat the oven to 200°C.

Scrub the potatoes with a 'green scratchy' (see page 4), but do not peel them. Cut each potato lengthwise into about 8 wedges and place them in a bowl of cold water as you go. Once all the potatoes have been scrubbed and chopped, drain off the water and pat the wedges dry.

Mix together the oil, soya sauce, garlic, parmesan cheese and salt in a shallow bowl. Using your fingers, gently turn the potato wedges in this mixture to coat. As each wedge is coated, stand it skin-side down on a shallow baking tray lined with a piece of baking paper.

Bake for 35–40 minutes or until the wedges are tender and golden brown.

VARIATIONS: Mix different seasonings with the oil. Use your favourites or try one or more of the following: curry powder, cumin, plain or smoked paprika, flavoured salts, crumbled dried oregano, thyme or sage.

Omit the parmesan cheese and sprinkle some grated cheddar cheese over each wedge a few minutes before they have finished baking.

Serve hot or warm with dips such as guacamole, salsa, satay sauce, or sour cream, as snacks or appetisers.

Skordalia

We've seen this delicious dish served in much the same way as mashed potatoes, but it is traditionally served as a dip.

FOR 4–6 SERVINGS:

4 medium (about 700g) all purpose or floury potatoes
6 cloves garlic
½ cup olive oil
6 Tbsp wine vinegar or a lemon juice and vinegar mixture
about ½ tsp salt
pinch of paprika to garnish, optional

Peel the potatoes. Gently boil until tender. Drain well, then mash.

Peel and finely chop or grind the garlic to a paste. Place the garlic, mashed potato, oil and vinegar in a food processor. Process until smooth, then season to taste with salt.

Garnish with the paprika if desired and serve immediately with vegetable crudités or refrigerate in a covered container until required.

Fat-Free Potato Wedges

These easy-to-prepare potato wedges make excellent, wonderfully easy and very popular snacks to serve alone, or with one or more dips, as a snack. They are best eaten as soon as they are cooked.

Preheat oven to 200–225°C, (fan-bake) with a rack in the middle of the oven.

Wash, rub with a "green scratchy" (see page 4) and dry several medium to large potatoes. For preference use evenly shaped, oval potatoes, each of which weigh 250–300g. (Agria are our favourites but you can use others too.)

Cut the potatoes lengthwise into six long wedges.

Lay each wedge, skin-side down, on an oven tray lined with baking paper, or a non-stick liner. Sprinkle the cut surfaces with pepper if you like, or leave them exactly as they are.

Bake for 60 minutes at the lower temperature, or 45 minutes at the higher temperature, until the wedges are an even light brown.

Serve the wedges hot, on paper napkins.

VARIATIONS: Cook the potato wedges exactly as above, and serve as a side dish, with meat and other vegetables.

Boiling and salad potatoes have a waxy texture which is smooth and holds together beautifully during cooking. All new potatoes come into this category. Other potatoes with this texture are Nadine, Draga, Frisia, and limited or local supplies of Jersey Benne, Liseta, Red King Edward, and Tiffany.

Baking, roasting and mashing potatoes have a soft, floury texture. Varieties include Ilam Hardy, Red Rascal, Agria, Fianna, and localised supplies of White Delight.

Some potato varieties fit somewhere between Waxy and Floury and are all-purpose potatoes. Look for Rua, Desiree, Karaka, and Moonlight, and limited and local supplies of Red Ruby, Rocket and Maris Anchor.

Potato Puffs

Potato puffs are small, tasty savouries that are always very popular for morning tea savouries, at parties, for suppers, and at 'ladies a plate' functions, as long as there is an oven in which they can be reheated. They are also enormously popular with hungry teenagers, and will disappear from the plate like magic if you are nice enough to make them for your children and their friends as an after-school treat. They are also very good served with soup at lunchtime.

We do, however, have to add a word of warning. Straight from the oven, they are dangerously hot and can burn the inside of your mouth! Leave them to cool a little before serving.

FOR 12 SAVOURIES:

3 slices sandwich bread
butter for spreading
1 cup cold mashed potato
1 cup grated tasty cheese
1 egg
1–2 Tbsp onion pulp (see below)
1–2 rashers bacon, chopped
salt or seasoned salt
pinch of paprika, optional

Lightly butter each slice of bread. Cut off the crusts if you are fussy, then cut each slice into four small squares. Press the squares into patty or muffin pans, butter-side down.

Preheat the oven to 190ºC.

Mix the mashed potato with the cheese, egg, onion pulp and bacon (the less bacon you use, the more salt you'll need).

Spoon the mixture into the uncooked bread cases (best done with two dessertspoons; use the tip of the second one to help slide the potato mixture off the first spoon). Sprinkle the potato mixture with a little paprika for extra colour if desired.

Bake for 20–30 minutes until the bread cases are light brown.

Eat when hot (but not too hot), or cool on a rack, then freeze for reheating later.

NOTE: To make onion pulp, cut an unpeeled onion through its equator, i.e. horizontally, then scrape the surface with the edge of an upside-down teaspoon.

VARIATION: Make four giant savouries, using four slices of bread to fill each of four round individual pie tins/moulds. Divide the potato filling between the four pie shells, and bake as above.

Swiss Potato Cake

We love this recipe and although Alison feels her untraditional version might well horrify a traditional Swiss cook, her family has always enjoyed it. For Alison, it brings back wonderful memories, when she and Peter enjoyed these cakes on a perfect summer's evening, on the top of a perfect Swiss mountain, outside a perfect Swiss chalet, surrounded by perfect Swiss cows. It could not have been nicer!

FOR 1 SERVING:

2 medium (about 300g) all purpose or floury potatoes, grated
about 25g butter, melted
about 2 tsp oil
about ½ cup grated cheese
2 tsp finely chopped herbs
½ cup sautéed mushrooms

Scrub and coarsely shred the potatoes with a sharp cutter, e.g. using the shredding blade in a food processor. Plunge the shreds into a bowl of cold water and leave for at least 5 minutes. Drain the shreds in a colander, then pat dry using folded paper towels or a clean teatowel.

Melt the butter in a large pot, then add the potato and toss to coat.

Heat the oil in a small non-stick frypan, ensuring the base and sides are well coated. Add the potato, pressing down on the mass quite firmly. Place the lid on the pan at an angle so it is ajar and cook over moderate heat for about 15 minutes or until the cake is evenly golden brown on the underside. Slide the cake out of the pan onto the lid or a plate, then flip it back into the pan, uncooked side down. Cook for a further 10 minutes, again with the lid ajar. During the last 3 minutes sprinkle over the grated cheese mixed with the herbs, top with the sautéed mushrooms, then let the cheese melt slightly. Slide the potato cake onto a plate, with the cheese and mushroom topping uppermost.

Serve immediately with a side salad, and a bread roll if desired.

Baked Baby Potatoes

Baked baby potatoes make an interesting and simple twist on finger food. They're delicious filled with a little blue cheese, or sour cream and chives, or sour cream and smoked salmon.

Brining the potatoes first may seem like an unusual step, but it's easy and really does give the skins a different texture.

For up to 1kg baby new potatoes, make a brine solution by dissolving 3 teaspoons of salt in 4 cups of hot water. Place the potatoes in a large bowl or pot, then pour the brine over them and leave them to stand for 30–60 minutes.

Preheat the oven to 180°C.

Drain the potatoes, then arrange them on a baking tray. Position the tray in the middle of the oven and bake for 30–40 minutes or until the potatoes are soft when gently squeezed.

Remove the potatoes from the oven, then leave them to stand until they are cool enough to handle.

Cut a cross in the top of each potato, then squeeze gently to open them up. Fill each with a small wedge of blue cheese or 1 teaspoon of sour cream, then top with a sprinkle of chives, a small piece of smoked salmon or even a small blob of salmon caviar.

Serve while still warm.

NOTE: While butter is always good with baked potatoes, it is best avoided if you plan to serve these as finger food as it becomes a little drippy when it melts.

Potato & Kumara Cakes with Mango Salsa

These crisp little potato and kumara cakes really come to life when served with this delicious mango salsa!

FOR 2–3 SERVINGS:

200g all purpose or floury potatoes
150g kumara
2 spring onions
1 large egg
½ tsp salt
black pepper
about ¼ cup oil for cooking

SALSA:

400g can mango slices in light syrup or 1 cup finely
    chopped fresh mango
1 spring onion
1 Tbsp lemon (or lime) juice
½ tsp minced red chilli
½ tsp salt
1–2 Tbsp chopped coriander leaf

Scrub the potatoes and kumara, then grate with the skins on. Place the grated mixture in a bowl and cover with water. Leave to stand for 1–2 minutes, then drain in a sieve, squeezing out as much water as you can. Transfer back to the dried bowl.

Thinly slice the spring onions and add these to the grated mixture along with the egg, salt and a generous grind of black pepper, then stir lightly with a fork to combine (do not over-mix). Leave the mixture to stand while you prepare the salsa.

Drain the mango slices and cut the flesh into 5mm cubes. Thinly slice the spring onion then mix this together with the cubed mango, lemon or lime juice, chilli, salt and chopped coriander in a small bowl.

Heat the oil in a large non-stick pan, gently drop generous dessertspoons of the kumara-potato mixture into the pan, flattening them into cakes about 1cm thick. Cook over a medium-high heat for 3–4 minutes per side, or until crisp and golden brown.

Drain the cooked cakes briefly on several layers of paper towels, then arrange on plates and serve topped with a generous dollop of the salsa and a green salad.

Did you know that Kiwis get around 30% of their vitamin C from potatoes?

Be creative with your toppings for baked or microwaved potatoes! As well as sour cream and grated cheeses, try lighter options of baked beans, chilli, tuna and salsa. Serve them with a salad as a complete meal!

Mediterranean Potatoes

This recipe turns everyday potatoes into something that will delight everyone. Depending on the flavourings added, the potatoes can be served on the side or as the main part of a casual meal.

FOR 2 MAIN COURSE SERVINGS:

6 medium (about 900g) all purpose or floury potatoes
2–3 Tbsp olive or other oil
1–2 large cloves finely chopped garlic
pinch of chilli powder or cayenne pepper
several sprigs of fresh thyme, rosemary and/or sage
½ tsp salt or 2 tsp chopped capers
1 Tbsp chopped anchovies
2 Tbsp caper vinegar
about ¼ cup chopped parsley
black olives, optional

Scrub the potatoes to remove all dirt, then cut them lengthwise into large chunky wedges or chip shapes. Rinse or stand in cold water for a few minutes before patting dry.

Heat the oil in a large frypan. Add the prepared potatoes and toss to coat evenly. Cover the pan and cook over a moderate heat, turning every 5 minutes for about 20 minutes until the potatoes are barely tender and are lightly browned on most sides.

After about 10 minutes stir through the garlic, then sprinkle the potatoes with chilli powder or cayenne pepper. Mix well. Add the herb sprigs and the salt or capers to the pan, then cover again.

When the potatoes are tender, remove the herbs. Mix in the anchovies and the caper vinegar and cook for about 10 minutes further, uncovered, turning occasionally. Taste and adjust the seasonings as desired.

Just before serving, mix through the chopped parsley. Pile the potatoes into a serving dish and scatter the olives – if using – over the top.

Serve with poached or fried eggs and a green salad or a chunky tomato and basil salad.

Bubble & Squeak

Alison and her sisters loved Bubble and Squeak when they were growing up. Their mother always cooked large amounts of potatoes and other vegetables to accompany the evening meal and leftovers would be stirred together before being put away in a cool place overnight.

Next morning, the vegetables would be mixed with a little milk, put into a preheated frying pan with a knob of butter, then pushed down to form a cake. As the mixture browned on both sides until it became crusty, the pan made popping noises (or bubbled and squeaked?) and the smell of browned potatoes became more and more inviting. Each serving was topped with a fried egg – the perfect accompaniment. But none of the girls put on weight, probably because as well as walking some distance to school every day, they would also play outside with their friends after school.

Although you may not want Bubble and Squeak for breakfast, it makes a good weekend lunch or easy dinner if you have the ingredients on hand. Quantities need not be precise, but the potatoes and cabbage are vital ingredients.

FOR 4 SERVINGS:

2–3 cups cooked potatoes, mashed or chopped
about 1 cup well-drained, shredded cooked cabbage
about 2 cups cooked or leftover vegetables, optional
milk to mix
2 Tbsp butter

Mix the mashed potatoes with the cabbage. Chop the vegetables into smallish pieces if using, then add to the potato. Mix well, adding a little milk if the vegetable mixture is too dry.

Heat a frypan, preferably with a non-stick finish. Add the butter and before it browns, tip in the vegetable mixture, firmly pushing it into the pan. Cook over a low to medium heat for about 10 minutes until the mixture is crusty and golden brown. Slide the mixture from the pan onto a plate, turn it back into the pan, browned-side up, and cook until the other side is browned, and it is hot in the middle.

To serve, cut into wedges and top with a fried egg if desired or with a mixed salad alongside.

VARIATION: Some older English recipes call for cold roast meat to be chopped and added to the uncooked mixture.

 Make potatoes one or more servings towards your "five plus vegetables a day".

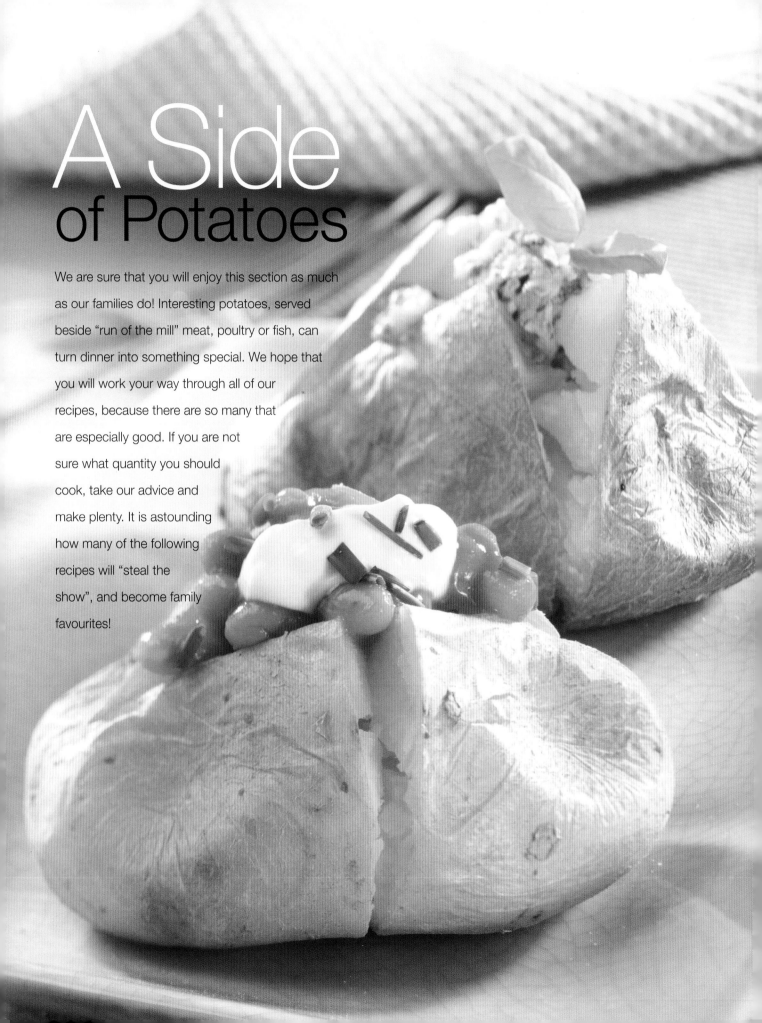

A Side
of Potatoes

We are sure that you will enjoy this section as much as our families do! Interesting potatoes, served beside "run of the mill" meat, poultry or fish, can turn dinner into something special. We hope that you will work your way through all of our recipes, because there are so many that are especially good. If you are not sure what quantity you should cook, take our advice and make plenty. It is astounding how many of the following recipes will "steal the show", and become family favourites!

How to Cook Potatoes

Here are the basic instructions for cooking potatoes absolutely plainly. You may like to refer to these outlines when making a recipe which tells you to start with cooked potatoes.

All Purpose and Floury Potatoes (plus 'Main Crop' Waxy Varieties)

- Wash or scrub the potatoes you are going to cook.

- Peel them thinly, using a sharp vegetable knife or a potato peeler, or rub them all over with a 'green scratchy' – a plastic pad with a rough texture, usually sold in bundles, and meant for cleaning food particles off pots. Scrubbing them like this is fast and there's much less wastage than when peeling potatoes, especially with a knife.

- Cut out and discard any damaged parts of the potato.

- Cut the peeled potatoes into even-sized pieces.

- Bring a pot of lightly salted water to the boil. Drop in all the potatoes and check that the water barely covers the potatoes. Cover with a lid so the potatoes are surrounded by water or steam.

- When the water returns to the boil, lower the heat so the water is simmering.

- Cooking time will vary – anything from 15–30 minutes – and will depend on the variety of potato used, their size and the heat source. Check by piercing a large piece of potato with the sharp point of a knife. The potato is cooked when there is little resistance.

- Drain the cooked potatoes, saving the cooking water for use in gravy, sauce or to add to a pot of soup. It is quite surprising how much flavour there is in potato cooking liquid.

Early Season Waxy or 'New' Potatoes

- Using a vegetable knife or 'green scratchy' (see above), scrape off the thin, delicate skin of new potatoes. Cut out any imperfections, leaving the potatoes whole if they are small or cutting them in pieces of similar size.

- Bring a pot of lightly salted water to the boil. Drop in all the potatoes and check that the water covers the potatoes. Cover with a lid so the potatoes are surrounded by water or steam.

- Add a little sugar, salt, garlic, some mint sprigs or herbs of your choice to the water.

- After the water boils, cook them at a gentle simmer until tender when pierced.

- Cooking time will probably be a little shorter than the time required for main crop potatoes. Drain the cooked potatoes, then turn them in a little melted butter. If you have cooked them with mint, you can serve the edible leaves with the potatoes.

Stove-Top Mashed Potatoes

Mashed potatoes are comfort food with a capital M! A pile of light, fluffy, creamy mashed potatoes can be the highlight of a meal, whether you are cooking for yourself, your family, or guests.

It's worth taking a little time and trouble over their preparation, so they finish up absolutely perfect.

Start with all purpose or floury potatoes, since new or waxy potatoes will not turn out to be fluffy.

Wash or scrub the potatoes you are going to cook. Cut them into even-sized pieces.

Bring a pot of lightly salted water to the boil. Drop in all the potatoes and check that the water barely covers the potatoes. Cover with a lid so the potatoes are surrounded by water or steam.

Drain the potatoes when they are tender right through when tested with a pointed knife. Pour off the cooking liquid, saving it for later use in a gravy or sauce. If you have time, allow the drained potatoes to stand in the dry pot for 2–3 minutes.

Mash with a potato masher or push the potatoes through a potato ricer. Add 1 teaspoon of butter per serving. Lastly, beat the mashed potatoes with a fork, adding milk until they are light, smooth and creamy. Season as needed.

Serve immediately or leave to stand in a warm place for a few minutes before serving.

Microwaved Mashed Potatoes

It is hard to give accurate timing for cooking potatoes in the microwave because of the difference in cooking time between potato varieties and the varying levels of power in microwave ovens. Keep a note of how long it takes to cook a certain weight of potatoes, especially if you buy in bulk. After a little experimenting and accurate timing, you should be able to produce consistently good results.

Cut peeled all purpose or floury potatoes in 1–2cm cubes and put them in a microwave bag, dish or bowl.

Add 1 teaspoon butter and 1 tablespoon water per serving.

Cover and cook at 100% power in a microwave oven for 2–3 minutes per serving, shaking to reposition the potato cubes about halfway through the cooking time.

Leave to stand for 5 minutes after cooking, then test to make sure all the cubes are cooked through completely.

Mash without draining, adding milk, salt and pepper to taste. Then beat with a fork until they are light, smooth and creamy.

NOTE: Should the potato cubes appear to be slightly shrunken when you check them after cooking, you have cooked them too long. Next time you cook the same variety, allow half a minute less per serving.

Oven-Baked Potatoes

Baked potatoes are easy to prepare and cook. They may be served plainly as part of a meal or stuffed with a variety of interesting fillings and served as the main part of a meal.

To Bake Traditionally: Scrub medium to large potatoes, then brush or rub with oil (this will keep the skins soft). Bake on a rack, rather than on a solid surface, in a preheated 200°C oven for 50–60 minutes or at 180°C for 60–75 minutes until the potato flesh gives when pressed.

Microwave-Baked Potatoes

Scrub medium to large potatoes (try to choose potatoes roughly the same size for even cooking), then prick each one several times before cooking. Turn potatoes over halfway through cooking time.

For 100g of potatoes allow 3 minutes at high power

For 200g of potatoes allow 5½ minutes at high power

For 300g of potatoes allow 7½–8 minutes at high power

For 400g of potatoes allow 10 minutes at high power

Leave microwaved potatoes to stand for 3–5 minutes then cut a cross in the top of each one. Press down gently between the cuts to open out the cross. Put a little butter, sour cream or cheese in the cut.

A small number of potatoes will microwave faster than boiled potatoes. However, it is easy to overcook them, in which case they will be slightly shrivelled. You can avoid this next time by cooking them for a shorter period.

NOTE: Cooking times will vary with different microwave ovens, depending on their wattage. Use less time if you have a high powered oven.

Slow Cooked Baked Potatoes

Did you know that you can cook baked potatoes in a slow cooker? It is very handy to be able to fill up your slow cooker with foil-wrapped potatoes in the morning, then return to the kitchen hours later to find them ready and waiting! It's so easy too – all you need are potatoes, some foil and, of course, a slow cooker.

Choose potatoes that are labelled as 'suitable for baking'. Larger potatoes will take longer to cook all the way through so for best results select potatoes of similar size.

Wrap as many as you will need individually in foil (to stop them drying out) and arrange them in the cooker. Cover, turn the slow cooker to LOW, and in 6–8 hours you should have delicious baked potatoes!

Serve the baked potatoes with butter and/or sour cream as a side dish. Or they can be stuffed, e.g. with baked beans and grated cheese, leftover mince mixtures, etc., and served as a main dish, in which case it is best to reheat them, either in a microwave or regular oven, until the filling is heated through.

Sometimes potatoes that have been pressed against the sides of the cooker bowl can brown a bit. To prevent this happening, turn or rearrange them after 4–5 hours.

Twice Baked Potato Skins

Twice baked potato skins were very popular some years ago. Although they are seldom seen in restaurants these days, they remain a delicious treat so why not make them at home. They offer plenty of scope to experiment with different spices and dips or toppings.

Cut as many baked potatoes as required into quarters lengthwise as soon as they are cool enough to handle. Scoop out most of the cooked flesh, leaving a 5mm shell. (Refrigerate the flesh to use at a later time.) Brush both sides of the skins with canola or olive oil, then sprinkle one side with salt, pepper, and two or three of your favourite dried spices.

Bake, uncovered, in a shallow metal dish, in a preheated 230°C oven for 15–20 minutes or until crisp and browned around the edges. Top with – or dip into – salsa, pesto, or grated cheese, etc.

Checkerboard Potatoes

Sometimes it's good to cook potatoes in a way that is just a little different. Checkerboard potatoes are worth trying – they cook more quickly than regular baked potatoes, they look more colourful and they don't require any last minute attention.

Scrub some fairly large, oval potatoes – as many as are required – and cut each one in half lengthwise. Using a sharp vegetable knife make a series of parallel cuts lengthwise, 5mm apart, cutting down as deeply as you can without cutting through the skin. Then cut similar lines crosswise so you finish up with a checkerboard design.

Blot the cut surface with a paper towel, pressing down firmly, then lightly brush the same surface with melted butter or oil. Sprinkle evenly with paprika. (You will get a nice even result if you shake the paprika through a fine sieve.)

Bake the potatoes, cut side up, in a preheated 200°C oven for 35–40 minutes or until the potatoes feel soft when squeezed. The cuts should open slightly during the cooking process. Serve immediately.

Roast Potatoes

Roasted potatoes that cook in a roasting pan with a joint of meat or a chicken need very little attention as they cook. They will brown better and crisp up more if they are not packed in the pan too tightly and are cooked in a large shallow roasting pan rather than in a small deep roasting pan. And because the roasting meat spatters a bit as it cooks, the potatoes get naturally basted. Then there are the pan drippings, which add flavour and colour to the potatoes.

Although large potatoes can be cut in half or into quarters for roasting, oval-shaped, whole, smallish potatoes look particularly good. We think the heat circulates round them better too, since only a small part of an oval potato lies against the roasting pan surface.

Main crop potatoes (see pages 5 & 93) take about 60–75 minutes at 180°C, depending on their size. We think it is a good idea to turn potatoes over occasionally, so they become golden brown and crisp on as many surfaces as possible.

NOTE: New potatoes do not roast well.

Crusty Roast Potatoes

Peel the required number of potatoes – main crop (see pages 5 & 93) are best – and cut them into even-sized pieces. Parboil (partly cook) in boiling water for 15 minutes.

Pat dry, coat lightly with flour then roast as above. Some people like to roughen the surface of the parboiled potatoes with a fork so they brown better, but it's not really necessary.

Garlic Roast Potatoes

Peel the required number of potatoes, ideally oval-shaped, smallish, whole potatoes.

Bring a pot of lightly salted water to the boil. Drop in all the potatoes and check that the water covers them. Cover and cook for 15 minutes.

Drain the potatoes, pat dry, then stand them on a board until they are cool enough to handle.

While the potatoes are cooking, mash 2 cloves of garlic in ¼ cup oil using a pestle and mortar or a small grinder or blender.

When the potatoes are cool enough to handle, make some deep crosswise cuts, 5mm apart, on each potato taking care not to cut them right through. Thoroughly brush each potato with the garlic oil, ensuring that the oil gets into the cuts.

Put the potatoes in a shallow baking dish and cook in an oven preheated to 200°C for about 1 hour, brushing with more garlic oil at intervals.

Cubed Roast Vegetables

A platter of seasoned roasted vegetables makes an interesting addition to almost any dinner. A good combination of vegetables includes some all-purpose potatoes, orange kumara, pumpkin, carrots, parsnip, beetroot, red onions, red, green and/or orange peppers, mushrooms, etc.

FOR 8 SERVINGS:

8–10 cups prepared vegetables (see above)
4 tsp garlic-infused or plain olive oil
handful of fresh rosemary leaves

Seasoning Mix:
1 Tbsp ground cumin
1 tsp each curry powder, plain or smoked paprika, celery salt and garlic salt
½–1 tsp chilli powder, optional

Combine all the ingredients for the seasoning mix into a screw-topped jar. Shake to mix.

Preheat the oven to 220°C.

Prepare the vegetables. Remove the skin from the pumpkin and onions and wash the other vegetables. Cut everything except the onions and mushrooms into 2–3cm cubes. Cut the onions into quarters through the root. Leave the mushrooms whole.

Put all the vegetables except the mushrooms in a large plastic bag (supermarket bags are good for this). Drizzle three-quarters of the oil over them, then toss to coat. Sprinkle into the bag about 3–4 teaspoons of the seasoning mix (save the rest for future use) and toss the vegetables again. Lastly, add the rosemary leaves and toss again. Brush the mushrooms with the rest of the oil.

Place a Teflon liner or some non-stick baking paper into each of two large roasting pans. Tip in the vegetables and spread them out so they are no more than two deep.

Bake for about 1 hour.

VARIATION: Toss in some chopped fresh herbs or toasted pinenuts, black olives or grilled cherry tomatoes after the vegetables have been roasted.

Bird's Nest Potatoes

This recipe has been popular with Alison's family for more than 40 years. A food processor makes light work of grating the raw potatoes and a large electric frypan will do a great job of cooking them (you need a large pan unless you are just cooking for one or two people).

Scrub, then grate 1 large all purpose or floury potato per person. Pile the shredded potato in the centre of a clean teatowel. Squeeze the teatowel to remove most of the liquid from the shredded potato. Heat a little canola or olive oil in a very hot frypan, then drop handfuls of potato into the pan. Flatten each 'cake' lightly, but do not pack the shreds too tightly. Turn the cakes over when they are golden brown, adding more oil when cooking the second side if necessary.

NOTE: Work fast, putting the grated potato into the pan soon after grating it or the raw potato will turn brown on standing.

Potatoes are easy to grow – see pages 92 and 93 for everything you need to know.

Kiwis love potatoes!

97% of New Zealanders eat potatoes

54% of the population eat fresh potatoes four or more times a week

42% of New Zealanders eat processed potatoes at home fortnightly or more

20% of the population eat fresh potatoes each day

New Zealanders eat 7 million portions of hot chips per week

Skillet Potatoes

These potatoes are always very popular. Our extended family thinks that they are particularly good served in warm weather, with cold meat and a tomato salad or a mixed salad. If you have an electric frypan with a non-stick finish, you will find the recipe is particularly easy to make, otherwise use a large frypan – but don't forget to keep an eye on the potatoes as they cook.

FOR 3–4 SERVINGS:

Scrub or peel 4–5 medium-size potatoes (about 600g). Cut the potatoes into 5mm thick slices and drop them into a bowl of cold water as you go.

Cook 2 sliced onions in 3–4 tablespoons butter (or 1 tablespoon each of butter and oil) in a large non-stick electric frypan with a lid.

Drain the raw potato slices, pat them dry and add to the onion in the pan. Turn to coat with butter, then cover and cook on low heat for 15 minutes, turning occasionally.

Uncover, then turn up the heat a little and allow the vegetables to brown slightly, cooking for a further 10–15 minutes.

Just before serving, drain off any excess butter/oil, season the potatoes with salt and pepper or any other seasonings you think would be good, and sprinkle with 2 tablespoons of finely chopped fresh herbs.

Sautéed Potatoes

Simple though they may be, sautéed potatoes are always really popular with everybody. Because of this, in our house we often cook more potatoes than we need for a meal – so there will be leftovers to sauté later on! Perfect, baby new potatoes are not suitable, but they are good after they have matured a bit and are not quite so waxy when cooked.

FOR 2 SERVINGS:

Slice 3–4 medium cold, cooked potatoes into chunky pieces. Heat 3–4 tablespoons of butter or oil (or a mixture of the two) in a non-stick frypan which is large enough for the potatoes to be easily turned. When the pan is hot, add the potatoes and cook, uncovered, turning every few minutes for 20–30 minutes until they are evenly crisp and golden. Sprinkle with chopped parsley before serving.

VARIATION: Bring to the boil in a small pot 2 tablespoons of wine vinegar, 1 chopped garlic clove, 1 teaspoon of finely grated lemon rind and 2 tablespoons of olive oil. Drizzle over the sautéed potatoes just before serving.

It pays to cook more potatoes than you need for dinner – for example, sauté leftovers for breakfast, or make a potato salad for lunch!

Potatoes of the same variety are not always identical. As a potato grows it is affected by the weather, climate, soil and the time of year.

Hash Browns

Alison and her family were first introduced to hash browns in San Francisco nearly 40 years ago. On their arrival they staggered off the plane with their two preschoolers, found a downtown hotel, and next morning went looking for a nearby place to eat breakfast. Alison suspects the dark-suited businessmen enjoying their quiet breakfast were not impressed with the family's rather noisy company, but all the Holsts thought the hash browns, bacon and 'easy over' fried eggs, cooked on a large hot plate in front of them were wonderful!

Boil or microwave as many large, floury potatoes as required until they are just tender (it's not necessary to peel them first). Refrigerate for at least 8 hours, then grate coarsely.

Heat a large frypan with just enough butter to form a film. When the butter is a light straw colour, spoon in the grated potatoes. Fill the pan to form a layer of potato about 2cm thick. Pat down evenly with a fish slice or turner so it forms a large, flat-topped cake. Brown over moderate heat for 10–15 minutes or until a crisp, golden brown crust forms underneath.

Slide the potato cake onto a plate, then flip it back into the pan, uncooked side down. Add a little extra butter down the sides of the pan and cook until crisp underneath.

Remove from the pan and cut into wedges. Serve with bacon, eggs, tomatoes, and/or mushrooms.

VARIATIONS:

Cook hash browns on a preheated, solid barbecue plate which has had a little oil drizzled onto it first. Hash browns are also popular when served with barbecued foods such as chops, steaks or sausages, with barbecued mushrooms and/or tomatoes and a green salad.

Shape then cook individual servings of hash browns if you are using a large square electric frypan.

NOTE: When we cook hash browns on a barbecue plate, we use oil instead of butter, keeping it in a squirt bottle for speed, accuracy and ease of use.

Potato Cakes

Deservedly popular, these potato cakes don't need much time nor do they need to be made to an exact formula – vary their seasonings and additions each time you make them, using what is available. You'll need to cook the cakes immediately because the mixture will turn sticky if left to stand.

FOR 1–2 SERVINGS:

1 cup grated or mashed cold cooked potato
½ cup self-raising flour or scone mix
½ tsp celery salt
½ tsp green herb instant stock powder
about 2 Tbsp chopped parsley or other herb/s
⅓–½ cup chopped cooked vegetables, chicken or meat, optional
milk
flour
oil

Mix the potato with the rest of the ingredients except the milk. Add enough milk to mix to a firm dough. Form into a cylinder on a wooden board, using a little flour to prevent the dough from sticking.

Cut into 1cm slices using a sharp serrated knife. Lightly flour both sides of each potato cake.

Pour the oil into a frypan to a depth of 5mm and heat. Cook the potato cakes in the hot oil for 4–5 minutes on each side until they are evenly browned. Do not shorten the cooking time or the centres of the potato cakes will be pasty.

Serve hot for breakfast or lunch or with salad or steamed vegetables for dinner.

VARIATIONS: Add the contents of a can of tuna or salmon, reserving the liquid. Omit the celery salt and instant stock powder and use the reserved liquid to mix the dough before adding any milk. For a milder flavour discard the liquid from the can and use flavourings and milk as above.

Potatoes are rich in vitamins and minerals, contain protective antioxidants and are virtually fat free.

Always remember how versatile potatoes are – they taste great when baked, stuffed, pan-fried, sautéed, roasted and barbecued, and of course, boiled then mashed! Yum!

Microwaved Cubed Potatoes

This is a very useful way to precook potatoes for salads and other recipes. Vary the seasonings and the size of the pieces to suit yourself.

The cubed potatoes will cook more quickly and evenly if they are coated with the oil or melted butter before they are microwaved.

PER SERVING:

1 medium waxy or all purpose potato, cubed
½ tsp butter or oil
2 tsp water
½ clove garlic, chopped, or 2 tsp chopped parsley, or
   1 chopped spring onion or 1 sprig of mint

Scrub or peel the potato. Cut into 1.5cm cubes, dropping them into a bowl of cold water as you go.

Drain the raw potato cubes and put in an oven bag or small microwave dish. Add the remaining ingredients, using oil if the potatoes are to be used in a salad. The potatoes will cook fastest and most evenly if they almost fill the container or bag they are in. If using an oven bag, loosely close it with a rubber band leaving a fingertip-sized gap through which steam can escape during cooking (without this gap, the bag may blow up and burst).

Approximate cooking times on 100% power:

1 serving (125–150g) 3–3½ minutes
2 servings (250–300g) 4–4½ minutes
4 servings (500–600g) 5–6½ minutes

After a couple of minutes of cooking, shake the container to coat the potato pieces evenly with the butter or oil and the seasonings.

Carefully squeeze the potatoes through the bag to see if they give a little to check if they are done.

Leave the potatoes to stand for 3–4 minutes after cooking.

NOTE: Should the potato cubes appear to be slightly shrunken when you check them, they have been overcooked. Next time you cook the same variety, allow half a minute less per serving.

Crunchy Brown Microwaved Potatoes

These are as close as we can get to fried potatoes using a microwave. You will need a microwave browning dish, which can sometimes be found in second-hand shops. These dishes are made by Corning, an American company, and they have a special coating on the bottom which gets very hot when it is heated in a microwave, allowing the potatoes to brown.

Change the seasonings to suit yourself, but a combination of curry powder and paprika results in a good colour.

FOR 2 SERVINGS:

2 medium (about 300g) all purpose or floury potatoes
1 Tbsp flour
1 tsp salt
1 tsp paprika
¼ tsp curry powder
1 Tbsp butter
1 Tbsp oil

Scrub or peel the potatoes. Cut into 1cm cubes, then pat dry with a paper towel. Measure the flour and seasonings into a dry plastic bag, shake to mix, then add the potato cubes and shake well to coat thoroughly.

Heat the empty browning dish on 100% power for 6 minutes. Have the butter and potatoes ready to go in as soon as the dish has heated.

As soon as the dish has finished heating, pour the oil into the dish without removing it from the microwave. Add the butter in several pieces, then quickly add the potatoes. Microwave, uncovered, at 100% power for 3 minutes. Again without removing the dish from the microwave, turn the potato using a spoon then cook for a further 2–3 minutes until a potato cube is tender when tested.

Serve hot as an accompaniment to a main meal or serve with pan-cooked bacon, tomato or mushrooms for a weekend breakfast or brunch.

Potatoes keep best in a cool place, out of direct light, in a ventilated paper or cardboard container, so you can buy enough for several weeks in large quantities.

When you make mashed potatoes, try different additions at times. Don't always use milk and butter! Try yoghurt or olive oil. Add extra flavours for a change – chopped fresh herbs, chopped spring onions, sautéed onions or sautéed chopped mushrooms.

Microwaved Herbed Potato Cake

This tasty and impressive dish is easy when made in a microwave oven, especially if you have a food processor and if you use a microwave ring pan.

FOR 4–5 SERVINGS:

about 25g butter
4 medium (about 600g) all purpose or floury potatoes
2 small onions or spring onions, very finely chopped
½ cup chopped fresh parsley or other fresh herbs
2 tsp instant green herb stock powder
½ cup grated cheese (mild or tasty to taste)
pinch of paprika

Melt the butter in a 6-cup microwave ring pan in which you will cook the potatoes.

Scrub the potatoes, ideally using a 'green scratchy' (see page 31). Coarsely shred the scrubbed potatoes, preferably using the shredding blade of a food processor, then place them in a bowl of cold water as soon as possible to prevent browning.

Drain the shredded potato in a sieve, squeezing them well to remove excess water (or pile the shredded potato in the centre of a clean teatowel, then gather up the edges and squeeze the teatowel to remove most of the liquid from the shredded potato).

In a bowl mix the potato with the onion, herbs, stock powder and the melted butter. Press the mixture into the microwave ring pan, cover with a lid or plastic film and microwave at 100% power for 10 minutes or until the potato cake is tender. Leave it to stand for 2 minutes, then turn it out onto a flat plate.

Scatter the grated cheese over the top, sprinkle with paprika and microwave for about 30 seconds or until the cheese melts.

Cut the potato cake into large chunky pieces and serve with meat or poultry and other vegetables.

NOTE: If you want to prepare this ahead of time, turn the cooked cake out onto a microwavable dinner plate, remove the centre cone, but leave the microwave dish over the potato cake on the plate. A few minutes before serving dinner, microwave it on 100% power until the cake is hot right through. Remove the dish before serving.

Microwaved Potatoes in Coconut Cream

Over the years Alison has made this recipe many times in various supermarkets. She is always surprised by the number of people who taste it and enjoy it so much that they rush off to buy the ingredients so they can make it themselves – as soon as they get home.

FOR 1–2 SERVINGS:

1 onion, chopped
4 small waxy or new potatoes (about 200g), unpeeled and cut into quarters
½–¾ cup canned coconut cream
1 tsp curry powder
¼ tsp salt
½ tsp sugar
1 cup frozen peas
about 100g cauliflorets, optional
1 cup chopped cabbage, optional

Put the onion and the potatoes in a microwaveproof dish with the coconut cream, curry powder, salt and sugar. (Use less coconut cream if peas are the only vegetable.)

Cover and microwave at 100% power for 5 minutes or until the potatoes are barely tender, then shake to mix.

Add the frozen peas and stir to coat the vegetables. Microwave for 3 minutes (use fewer peas if you are also adding cauliflower and cabbage but cook for 5 minutes, rather than 3), stirring at least once during the cooking time.

When the cauliflower and cabbage are cooked to the tender-crisp stage, taste and adjust the seasonings as required.

Serve immediately or leave to stand and reheat when required. This easy vegetable curry is good served alone or with grilled or barbecued meat or chicken.

NOTE: Alison uses new potatoes from her garden in summer, or small, pearly white Nadine potatoes at other times.

Buy smaller cans of coconut cream or look for dried coconut cream which can be reconstituted.

A microwaved potato cooks quickly and easily. Split it and add a topping of salsa and cottage cheese or tomatoes and tuna and you have an almost instant, low fat meal, at home or in the lunchroom at work!

A microwaved or baked potato in its skin contains more fibre than two slices of wholemeal bread.

Scalloped Potatoes

Although we often use the microwave oven to make scalloped potatoes for two, we tend to cook a family-sized dish in the oven, often alongside a meat loaf or similar. If you aren't in the habit of making scalloped potatoes, do try this recipe because we think it will win you over!

FOR 4 SERVINGS:

600g medium all purpose or floury potatoes
2 Tbsp (25g) butter
1–2 cloves garlic or 2 small onions, finely chopped
1 tsp salt
pepper to taste
1 cup milk

Preheat the oven to 200–220°C, positioning the rack just above the centre. (Set the temperature to 220° if you plan to cook something else at the same time; 200° if the potatoes will be on their own.)

Choose even shaped potatoes which will look more attractive when layered and thinly peel or scrub them with a 'green scratchy' (see page 4). Cut the potatoes into thin crosswise slices, and put them in a bowl of cold water.

Lightly coat the inside of a shallow ovenware dish with non-stick spray.

Heat the butter in a small pot, but don't let it brown. Add the garlic, stirring until it heats through. Add the salt, pepper and milk.

While the milk heats, drain the potatoes and arrange them in the prepared dish. Flatten them with your hand or with a fish slice top, then evenly pour over the hot milk mixture.

Cover with a lid, a sheet of foil or baking paper folded over loosely at the edges, and bake for 20–30 minutes. Uncover, and bake for a further 15–30 minutes until the top is golden brown, and the potatoes feel tender when pierced with a sharp knife.

Serve with a meat loaf, chops or sausages, etc., and vegetables.

Microwaved Scalloped Potatoes For Two

This remarkably good, quick and easy (taking less than 20 minutes from start to finish) dish looks impressive, and is sure to stand you in good stead on those occasions when you want to turn an ordinary meal into something much nicer!

FOR 2 SERVINGS:

2–3 medium all purpose or floury potatoes (about 300–450g)
1 small onion, thinly sliced
1 clove garlic, chopped, optional
2 tsp butter
1 Tbsp water
1 Tbsp flour
½ cup milk
flavoured or plain salt, e.g. celery, onion or garlic
½ cup grated cheddar cheese
1 Tbsp chopped parsley
about ¼ tsp paprika

Scrub the potatoes and cut them into 5mm thick slices. Combine with the onion and garlic and place in layers in a 20cm microwaveproof shallow casserole dish.

Add the butter and water, cover, and cook at 100% power for 5 minutes until the potatoes are barely tender, shaking the dish after 2–3 minutes.

Remove the dish from the microwave and sprinkle with the flour. Add the milk, and a little salt. Shake the dish or turn the potatoes over several times to mix the ingredients. Cover and cook for a further 2–3 minutes until the sauce thickens and the potatoes are perfectly tender.

Remove from the microwave again and sprinkle the top layer evenly with the cheese, parsley and paprika. Microwave, uncovered for about 1 minute or less until the cheese melts.

Serve with grilled meat and plainly cooked vegetables.

 Potatoes are really versatile – big piles of creamy mashed potatoes will be "wolfed down" in student flats, and duchesse potatoes (also made from mashed potatoes) can grace the most elegant dinner parties!

Easy Oven-Baked 'Chips'

Deep-frying chips happens very rarely in either of our households. We're not comfortable with the high fat content, we don't like clearing up the mess made by oil spattered over the stove as the chips cook, and we hate getting rid of the large quantities of stale oil involved. We have solved the problem by baking chips rather than frying them, which uses much less oil and makes very little mess. These baked chips always disappear very quickly, and as we don't get any complaints we feel that our families are hardly disadvantaged!

P.S. Just before the chips are done, we sometimes cut fish fillets into strips, dip them in flour, then into a beer batter made by mixing together 1 egg, ½ cup each of beer and flour, with seasonings to taste, and cook them in a pan of hot oil 2–3cm deep, turning them once.

FOR 2–3 SERVINGS OF CHIPS:

Preheat the oven to 230°C, positioning the tray in the centre.

Peel or scrub 2–3 large all purpose or floury potatoes and thinly slice into 5–7mm thick chips. Drop the chips into a bowl of cold water as you go and leave them to stand in the water for 5 minutes after you have finished to avoid browning.

Rinse the potatoes under cold running water, then thoroughly pat or blot them dry, using a clean teatowel or paper towels. Dry the bowl, too.

Return the chips to the dry bowl and pour 2–3 tablespoons of canola or other flavourless oil over them and mix with your fingers until they are completely coated with a thin film of oil.

Line a roasting pan or sponge roll tin with baking paper. Place the chips in the dish in one layer.

Bake in a preheated 230°C oven for 20 minutes until the chips are tender, turning once. If they do not brown enough in this time, slide out the baking paper and brown the chips under the grill.

Just before serving, sprinkle the chips with a little plain or seasoned salt. Serve immediately.

Sinfully Good Potato Wedges

These rich but absolutely delicious potatoes should be served only as an occasional treat. Coated with a heavily herbed and spiced mixture and baked until crisp, they are wonderful! We wouldn't feel so guilty eating them if we could stop after a couple, but (for us at least) it's impossible.

It is a good idea to line your baking dish with a non-stick Teflon liner or with baking paper so that the edges of the liner go up the sides a little. This will stop the wedges from sticking and make the clean-up minimal.

FOR 3–4 SERVINGS:

4 large (about 1kg) all purpose or floury potatoes
25g butter, melted
½ tsp salt
3 Tbsp olive oil
2 tsp finely chopped garlic
2 tsp ground cumin
1 tsp dried oregano
¼–½ tsp chilli powder

Scrub, then microwave or boil the potatoes whole until they are barely tender. Cool them if you have time, then cut each one lengthwise into 8 wedges.

Preheat the oven to 180°C.

Warm the butter in a large roasting pan until it is liquid but not hot. Add the salt, olive oil, garlic, cumin, oregano and chilli and mix well.

Using your hands, turn the potato wedges in the pan, mixing gently but thoroughly until all surfaces are well coated. Spread them out in a single layer, then bake for 1–1½ hours until crispy, turning once.

VARIATION: Vary the amounts and types of herbs and spices to suit yourself.

Serve warm, as a snack, for dipping into your favourite tomato-based salsa (or with the delicious green pea pesto from our Diabetes book).

 Not sure how much a serving of potatoes (and other vegetables) is? It's about a handful – how easy is that to remember!

Nelson Potatoes

This is a really good recipe that Alison dreamed up one stormy night in a motel in Collingwood after a very long drive with two pre-teens in the back seat. They had hoped to feast on fresh fish from fishing boats, but it was not to be. They dashed out, bought sausages, apples and apple cider, shut themselves in their motel, forgot about the weather outside, and had a very good time (probably because she and Peter drank the rest of the cider instead of having any green vegetables!)

You should always cook much more of this mixture than you think you need because it disappears so fast!

FOR 4 SERVINGS:

2 medium onions
2 Tbsp butter or oil
3 medium Granny Smith or Braeburn apples
3 large (about 600g) all purpose or floury potatoes,
    scrubbed and sliced
½ cup liquid such as apple juice, cider, stock or wine
freshly ground pepper and salt
chopped fresh herbs, e.g. sage, thyme or oregano

Peel and slice the onions. Cook them in a large frypan in the butter or oil until they are transparent and browned on the edges. Raise the heat, add the sliced apples and cook, uncovered, stirring often, until the apples have also slightly browned.

Mix in the sliced potatoes, then add the liquid. Cover tightly and cook for about 20 minutes until the potatoes are tender. Lift the lid from time to time and turn the apples and vegetables, adding extra liquid if the mixture becomes too dry.

Add pepper, salt and herbs to taste just before serving.

Served with sausages or pork chops, this combination is especially good, but we like it with any grilled meat as well as ham and smoked chicken.

Duchesse Potatoes

These potatoes always look impressive, and can be served alongside most meat, poultry or fish dishes for special occasions. They are made by adding egg to firm, lump-free mashed potatoes, which can then be piped into any shape you like, e.g. large rosettes or circular nests which can then be filled with a colourful vegetable mixture. Another attractive option is to pipe the potato mixture around the edge of scallop shells or individual dishes of similar size which you can later fill with seafood in a creamy sauce. For best results use floury potatoes.

Duchesse potatoes can be prepared ahead, browned attractively in the oven, and reheated in a low oven just before serving. However, it is really important to ensure that the mashed potato mixture is completely smooth – any lumps can block the piping bag. To make lump-free mashed potato, use a potato ricer (a metal cylinder with holey sides – a bit like a giant garlic crusher), available from most speciality kitchen shops. Fill it with boiled, floury potatoes, then put the presser in place and push down until all the potato has been squeezed out the small holes. If you do not want to invest in a potato ricer, simply press the cooked potatoes through a sieve to get rid of any lumps – it takes a bit longer, but it works!

For 4 servings, peel and chop 500g floury potatoes into even-size pieces. Boil until tender, but not mushy. Press the drained, cooked potato through a sieve or potato ricer, then mash with 25g butter and 1 large beaten egg (and an extra yolk if possible). Keep the mixture firm. Season to taste, then transfer the mashed potatoes into a forcer bag

with a star-shaped nozzle. Pipe out the mixture into shapes of your choice on to a sheet of baking paper on a baking tray, e.g. rosettes or circles that can later be filled with a vegetable mixture.

Bake the piped shapes in a preheated 200ºC oven for 20 minutes or until the edges turn brown.

NOTE: The rosettes always spread a little when they are baked.

Party Potatoes

Here is a shortcut recipe that is ideal for those times when you have to prepare a meal for a crowd. The buttery herbed coating disguises the flavour and appearance of the canned potatoes. Allow about 2–3 potatoes per person, depending on the age and appetites of your guests.

FOR 40 SERVINGS:

about 15 x 410g cans of small potatoes
6–8 Tbsp melted butter
about 1 cup finely chopped fresh herbs, e.g. a
    combination of parsley, chives, thyme and oregano,
    or parsley, chives and dill (chop herbs in food
    processor for best results)

Drain the potatoes from the cans, reserving the liquid. Put them in a covered microwave dish or in a large oven bag with ½ cup of the reserved liquid and heat at 100% power for 9–10 minutes. If using an oven bag, use a rubber band rather than a metal twist to loosely seal it.

Drain the potatoes, turn them in a third of the melted butter, then sprinkle generously with about ¼ cup of the herbs. Mix gently to coat evenly.

Repeat this process with the remaining potatoes.

If it is not possible to microwave the potatoes just before you need them, microwave them ahead of time then put them while they are still hot in oven bags and place the bags in an insulated container, e.g. a chilly bin, for up to 1 hour. Transfer the prepared potatoes to serving dishes just before they are required.

Serve as part of a buffet meal, as you would freshly cooked new potatoes. Use leftovers in potato salads, in scalloped potato dishes, or as sautéed potatoes.

NOTES: You can buy large catering-size cans of vegetables from cash-and-carry outlets. If you can get these, use 2–3 x 3kg size cans of potatoes in brine instead of the smaller cans. Large cans each contain about 45 small potatoes.

410g cans each hold about 6 fairly small potatoes – enough for two fairly generous servings.

Leftover canned potatoes may be refrigerated in plastic bags for 3–4 days.

Cooked potatoes should never be left standing around for long without refrigeration, especially in warm weather.

Friggione

This is a great vegetable mixture which you can make in the morning and bring out to serve with barbecued meat on a warm summer evening. For this to be at its best, do not scrimp on the cooking time. And although it loses its bright colour, it tastes better as the liquid disappears and the mixture darkens in colour.

FOR 4–6 SERVINGS:

about ¼ cup olive oil
5 medium (about 750g) all purpose or floury potatoes,
    scrubbed
2 large red onions
2 red and yellow peppers
1 x 425g can Italian seasoned tomatoes
1–1½ tsp salt
1 tsp sugar
freshly ground black pepper
chopped parsley, optional

Heat the oil in a large frypan, preferably with a non-stick surface. Cut the scrubbed potatoes into 1cm cubes and slice the onion and peppers.

Add the prepared potato, onion and pepper combination to the hot oil. Cover and cook over a moderate heat for 20 minutes, stirring several times, until the vegetables are tender and lightly browned.

Add the tomatoes and their juice. Cook, uncovered, over a medium heat for 15–30 minutes until the mixture darkens in colour and the liquid has reduced to just a small amount around the vegetables. Season to taste and sprinkle with the chopped parsley, if using, before serving.

Serve warm or hot, or reheat later in the frypan or in a microwave oven. Serve with barbecued meat, crusty rolls and a leafy green salad.

 Have you ever wondered why nutritionists are impressed by potatoes? It's because they contain Vitamin C, potassium, iron, magnesium, B group vitamins, antioxidants, fibre and carbohydrates!

Filo Surprise Packages

The potatoes on your dinner plate gain new importance when they are enclosed in crisp filo pastry! Make edible ties from long chive leaves or bacon or ham rinds to wrap up the packages but if this is not possible use string, in which case it should be removed before serving.

FOR 2 SERVINGS:

2 medium waxy or all purpose potatoes (about 300g), cooked
2 Tbsp sour cream or grated cheese
1–2 tsp fresh chopped herbs
¼ tsp salt
4 sheets filo pastry
edible ties or string (see above)

Slice the potatoes and mix with the sour cream, herbs and salt, varying the proportions to taste.

Preheat the oven to 180–190ºC.

Lay two of the filo sheets on a clean dry surface. Brush each of these lightly with oil or melted butter, then cover each with a second sheet of filo. Cut each of the sandwiched sheets in half cross-ways giving four, almost square sheets. Stack the 'sandwiches' so you have two piles, four layers thick, turning the top layer so that each stack resembles an eight pointed star. Pile the potato mixture in the middle, then gather up all four corners to enclose the potato. Tie up the corners with your choice of fastening so the package looks like a pouch. Gently fan out the corners.

Place the packages in a buttered sponge roll tin, then bake for 20–30 minutes until evenly browned.

Salmon Surprise Packages

Serve these filo packages as a light lunch for two with an interesting green salad that includes dill leaves and cucumber or with lightly cooked, buttered asparagus spears.

Follow the recipe for Filo Surprise Packages (see above), but use fresh dill or spring onion as the herb.

Cut into small pieces 4–6 slices of smoked salmon and 2 slices of brie or camembert cheese. Fold these extra ingredients through the rest of the filling along with 2 teaspoons of horseradish sauce.

Colcannon

Although we enjoyed our original colcannon recipe, made by stirring lightly cooked cabbage through mashed potatoes flavoured with a little nutmeg, we have now decided that we like it even better with sizzled bacon and bacon drippings stirred through.

Potatoes (all purpose or floury)
Cabbage
Salt
Butter
Bacon
Oil
Milk
Nutmeg

Cook potatoes in the usual way (see page 31).

When the potatoes are about half cooked, put the tender young cabbage which has been cut in 5mm slices, then

cut crosswise into fairly short lengths in a large frypan (in which you will later cook the bacon). Add a little salt and just enough butter (about ¼ teaspoon per serving) to stop the cabbage burning. Cover tightly and cook on high heat, watching until it is tender but still bright green, and all the water has evaporated. Set aside in a sieve.

Chop the bacon (one or two rashers per person) and put it in the pan in which the cabbage was cooked with 1 teaspoon of oil. Heat gradually over low heat, then raise the heat as bacon fat forms in the pan.

Meanwhile, drain and mash the potatoes. Add a little butter, some milk, pepper and freshly grated nutmeg. Beat with a fork until creamy and smooth.

When the bacon is light brown and crunchy, add the mashed potatoes and cabbage to the pan, and fold together. Taste and adjust the seasonings as required, then serve with baked or roast chicken or grilled sausages, etc.

Berrichonne Potatoes

These are so good we would almost eat them as a meal in themselves, but they also make a delicious side dish.

Effectively the potatoes are braised as they cook, which means they are a wonderful combination of soft and moist with brown crispy tops. Yum!

FOR 4–6 SERVINGS:

1 Tbsp olive or other oil
1 medium onion, peeled and diced
4–5 bacon rashers (about 125g), chopped
1kg all purpose or floury potatoes
1 tsp instant chicken stock powder
¾ cup hot water
2–3 Tbsp olive oil, extra
pepper to taste
¼ cup hot water, extra

Preheat the oven to 200°C.

Heat the first measure of oil in a large frypan. Add the onion and cook, stirring occasionally, until the onion has softened, then add the bacon. Continue to cook, stirring frequently until the bacon begins to brown, then remove the pan from the heat.

Scrub the potatoes well using a 'green scratchy' (see page 4). Quarter them lengthwise, then cut the quarters in half crosswise.

Coat the inside of a shallow 3 litre casserole dish with nonstick spray. Sprinkle the cooked onion and bacon into the dish, then scatter the potatoes over. Dissolve the stock powder in the first measure of hot water, then pour it over the potatoes. Drizzle the surface with the remaining measure of oil, and add pepper to taste.

Place the potatoes in the oven and bake for 40–45 minutes, gently turning the potatoes once after about 30 minutes. If the mixture begins to look too dry, add the extra hot water.

When the potatoes are golden brown and tender, remove from the oven and leave to stand for 5 minutes before serving.

Curried New Potatoes

Serve new potatoes in a curry sauce alongside grilled chops, pan-cooked sausages or a plain steak to make your meal more interesting.

FOR 4 SERVINGS:

2 Tbsp butter
1–2 tsp curry powder or to taste
1 onion, chopped
6 medium (about 600g) new or waxy potatoes
1 tsp instant chicken or vegetable stock powder
1 tsp sugar
½ cup hot water
½ cup coconut cream or ¼ cup sour cream
extra water if needed
½ cup thawed green peas, optional
¼ cup sour cream, optional
4–6 hardboiled eggs, optional
freshly chopped coriander leaves, optional

Melt the butter in a medium frypan. Add the curry powder and onion and cook gently for a few minutes.

Scrape or thoroughly scrub the potatoes, then cut into halves or quarter them lengthwise for quicker cooking. Add to the curry mixture, along with the instant stock and sugar dissolved in the hot water, and the coconut cream. Cover tightly and gently simmer for 15 minutes or until the potatoes are tender and the liquid is thick. Add extra water or raise the heat so you finish up with sauce thick enough to coat the potatoes.

Serve beside the plainly cooked meat or proceed as below.

VARIATION: Add ½ cup thawed green peas when the potatoes are nearly done, and cook until the peas are tender. If using sour cream rather than coconut cream, the sauce will be thinner. Cook uncovered until the sauce thickens to the desired consistency.

MAIN COURSE VARIATION: To make a main course for 2–3 people, make the sauce using the coconut cream. Add 4–6 hard-boiled eggs, sliced lengthwise, cut side up. Heat them through, covered, over very low heat. Serve the curried potatoes, peas and eggs on rice. Sprinkle with the coriander leaves if using.

NOTES: Do not use both sour cream and coconut cream.

Joginder Kaur Basi's Dry Potato Curry

This delicious curried potato recipe was given to Alison for use in this book by an experienced Indian cook who, with her daughters, set up Aashiayana, one of New Zealand's first Indian restaurants, in the late 1970s. We feel very honoured to have been given this recipe to share – over the years many people have asked for it but up until now, it has never been put to paper.

FOR 4 SERVINGS:

6 medium (about 600g) all purpose or floury potatoes
2 Tbsp vegetable oil or ghee
½ tsp asafoetida, optional*
1 Tbsp sesame seeds
1 Tbsp coriander seeds
1 Tbsp cumin seeds
4 garlic cloves, peeled but left whole
2–3cm piece root ginger, finely chopped or grated
2 green chillies, deseeded and finely chopped, optional
1 tsp sugar
1 tsp salt
1 Tbsp turmeric
1 tsp lemon juice
1 tsp garam masala
2 Tbsp fresh coriander leaves, chopped

*asafoetida is a spice with a rather strong odour, mainly used in Indian cooking. You may need to look in a speciality store for this.

Peel or scrub the potatoes and cut into 1.5cm cubes. Set aside.

Heat the oil in a large frypan with a lid. Add the asafoetida, if using, and brown for about 30 seconds over moderate heat.

Stir in the seeds and cover the pan until you hear the seeds begin to pop. Remove the lid and add the garlic, ginger, chilli if using, and the potato, sugar, salt and turmeric. Stir well. Reduce the heat to low, cover and cook for 10 minutes. Add the lemon juice, cover again, and cook for a further 10–20 minutes until the potatoes are tender. Stir in the garam masala and sprinkle with the coriander.

Serve with another curry, a salad if desired, and with naan or other Indian bread.

When you roast potatoes, spray them with a light but even oil coating rather than standing them in an oil bath!

Spicy Potatoes

A great accompaniment for any Indian-style meal, these look more complicated to make than they actually are. Curry leaves, which can sometimes be found in the produce department of your supermarket (and keep well frozen in an airtight bag) make an interesting addition if you can get them, but they're not essential.

FOR 4 SERVINGS:

600–800g waxy or all purpose potatoes
1 tsp turmeric
1 tsp salt
2 Tbsp canola oil
1 tsp mustard seed
1 tsp cumin seeds
1 tsp each paprika, ground coriander and garam masala
handful of curry leaves, optional
½–1 tsp minced red chilli, optional
2 Tbsp lemon juice
salt to taste

Scrub the potatoes and cut into 2cm cubes. Place them in a large pot and add just enough hot water to cover, then add the turmeric and salt. Bring to the boil and cook for 8–10 minutes until tender. Drain well and set aside.

Heat the oil in a large non-stick frypan. Add the mustard and cumin seeds and cook until the seeds begin to pop. Stir in the cooked potato, ground spices, curry leaves and chilli if using, and the lemon juice. Cook for 4–5 minutes, stirring frequently.

Remove from the heat, season to taste and serve immediately.

Greek-style Garlic & Lemon Potatoes

It's amazing how the flavours and aromas of food can bring the memories flooding back. The smell of these potatoes always evokes for Simon vivid memories of the Greek beach where he first tried these. They make a great accompaniment for fish or chicken dishes.

FOR 3–4 SERVINGS:

1kg all purpose or floury potatoes
2 cloves garlic, crushed
½ cup chicken stock
1–2 Tbsp lemon juice
2–3 Tbsp olive oil
salt and pepper to taste

Preheat the oven to 225°C.

Scrub the potatoes and cut into 2cm cubes. Coat the inside of a shallow 20 x 30cm casserole dish with non-stick spray. Add the potatoes, garlic, stock, lemon juice and the oil, then toss gently to combine. Season to taste with the salt and pepper.

Place the dish in the middle of the oven and cook for 20–25 minutes until golden brown, turning the potatoes gently once after about 10 minutes.

 Leave the skin on potatoes used for roasting, boiling, or in salads! You can even mash potatoes with their skin on – then you can be trendy and call them "smashed" potatoes!

Potato Gnocchi

These little potato gnocchi (Italian-style dumplings) are moist and delicious, with just a hint of nutmeg – serve them tossed in melted butter and topped with freshly grated parmesan cheese.

FOR 4–6 SERVINGS:

3 medium (750g) all purpose or floury potatoes
1 egg
½ tsp salt
¼ tsp freshly ground nutmeg
freshly ground black pepper
1–1½ cups flour
flour for dusting
knob of butter
freshly grated parmesan cheese
freshly chopped herbs to garnish

Microwave or boil the whole unpeeled potatoes until cooked but still firm. Drain and cool enough to handle.

Halve the potatoes and scoop out the flesh from the skins. Place the flesh in a large bowl or food processor. Mash or briefly process until lump-free.

Add the egg, salt, nutmeg and pepper to taste. Measure in 1 cup of flour, then mix together to form a smooth non-sticky dough. If it seems too wet, add a quarter cup more flour and mix again, adding more flour if necessary.

Knead the dough for about 1 minute, then divide it into four roughly equal balls. Roll the balls into 35–40cm long and 1.5cm thick lengths. Using a sharp knife, cut the dough into a number of smaller lengths measuring about 2.5–3cm. Shape by rolling each small piece lightly under your fingers, then pressing it against the back of a grater or rolling it under the tines of a lightly floured fork. Arrange the prepared gnocchi on a floured baking sheet or tray.

Bring a large pot of water to the boil. Tip 20 or so gnocchi into the water and boil for 2–3 minutes until they rise to the surface. Leave in the water for a further 30 seconds, then remove with a slotted spoon. Transfer the cooked gnocchi to a prewarmed dish and place the butter on top. Cook the remaining gnocchi in several batches, adding them to the warmed dish and tossing them in the melted butter as they are done.

Serve on warmed plates and top with parmesan cheese and the herbs if using.

Potato Bread

If you like to make bread, you may like to try this recipe. The addition of potato makes it seem more substantial, and it also helps to hold in moisture, keeping the bread fresh for longer.

MAKES A LARGE COTTAGE LOAF:

3 tsp Surebake yeast
1¾ cups warm water
3 Tbsp lecithin granules or oil
1 Tbsp sugar
1½ tsp salt
1 cup wholemeal flour
2 cups high-grade flour
1 cup instant potato flakes

Bread Machine Instructions: Carefully measure all the ingredients in the order specified by the manufacturer into a 750g capacity bread machine.

For a cooked loaf, set the machine to the NORMAL/WHITE bread cycle, MEDIUM crust and START, (or set to the DOUGH cycle, then shape, rise and bake the loaf by hand as described below.)

Hand-made Bread Instructions: Measure the first six ingredients into a large bowl and mix thoroughly. Cover and leave for 15 minutes or longer in a warm place.

Stir in the flour and potato flakes and stir to make a soft dough, adding a little extra flour if necessary, to make a dough which is just firm enough to turn out and knead.

Knead using the dough hook of an electric mixer or by hand on a lightly floured surface for 10 minutes, adding extra flour if necessary, until the dough forms a soft ball that springs back when gently pressed.

Turn the dough in 2–3 teaspoons of oil in a clean, dry bowl, then cover with plastic film and leave in a warm, draught-free place for 30 minutes.

Shaping and Baking: Knead the oiled dough lightly in the bowl for 1 minute, then turn out on a Teflon or baking paper-lined oven tray. Gently form into a large ball and leave to rise again in the same warm draught-free place for about 1 hour or until the dough has doubled in size.

Preheat the oven to 225°C. Lightly spray the top of the loaf with water and evenly sprinkle it with flour. Using a very sharp knife, make several shallow, parallel cuts about 2cm apart across the top of the loaf, then repeat this action at right angles to the original cuts to make a checkerboard pattern.

Bake for 20–30 minutes or until the loaf is evenly browned top and bottom, and sounds hollow when the bottom is tapped.

NOTE: Leave to cool before eating as the potato flakes can impart an unusual flavour which disappears on cooling.

Mainly Potatoes

Have fun with the recipes in this section, where potatoes are generously used in the main meal of the day. Many of these ideas come into the "Comfort Food" category. There are pies that are perfect for picnics or packed lunches, some of our favourite fish and potato dishes, and a good range of aromatic, bubbling casseroles to welcome family members when they come home at the end of a cold day. We hope you will try them all!

Minted Green Pea & Potato Frittata

This easy-to-make frittata is baked rather than cooked in a frypan, so you don't need to worry about it browning too much on the bottom as it cooks. It makes wonderful picnic food, is excellent for packed lunches for work or school, and is also popular as an informal weekend evening meal, served with a salad.

FOR 4–6 SERVINGS (12 SLICES):

500–600g new potatoes or washed white waxy potatoes
2 cups frozen minted peas
2–3 spring onions, finely sliced
4 medium firm tomatoes, deseeded and chopped into
    1cm cubes
2 cups grated tasty cheese
4 large eggs
1 cup evaporated milk
1 tsp salt
pepper to taste

Line a rectangular metal baking pan, about 20 x 30cm with sides about 5–6cm tall, with a sheet of baking paper. The paper should fit neatly in the base of the pan and up the sides, with the corners folded (but not cut). Coat the baking paper with non-stick spray.

Preheat the oven to 220°C (or 210°C fanbake) with the rack positioned in or just below the middle.

Scrape the new potatoes, or rub them if they are the white variety, then cut in half lengthwise, then in quarters crosswise. Cook in about 2cm of lightly salted water in a medium-sized pot, covered, for about 20 minutes or until the potatoes are almost tender. Add the peas and cook for

5–10 minutes longer. Drain the vegetables and spread them out on a shallow tray or dish to cool.

When the potatoes are cool enough to handle, cut the quarters into small chunks. Mix together the spring onion, tomato, peas and potatoes, then spread half the vegetable mixture over the paper-lined base of the pan. Sprinkle over half the cheese, then top with the remaining vegetable mixture.

In a bowl beat together the eggs, milk, and salt and pepper to taste. Pour evenly over the vegetable and cheese layers and sprinkle the remaining cheese over the top.

Bake for 40–45 minutes until the egg mixture is set and the cheese topping has browned attractively. Leave to cool for at least half an hour before cutting with a serrated knife into about 12 slices, three portions crosswise and four lengthwise.

Eat immediately or cover and refrigerate for up to two days until required.

VARIATIONS:

Add chopped ham or cooked chicken to the prepared vegetable mixture.

Replace the peas with mixed frozen vegetables adding any suitable chopped fresh herbs to replace the mint flavour.

Replace the chopped tomatoes with 1 or 2 chopped red peppers, and add them to the partly cooked potatoes with the peas.

NOTE: Using evaporated milk gives body and extra richness to the frittata.

Twice-Baked Stuffed Potatoes

As well as making a substantial meal, this recipe also lends itself to many different and tasty versions.

FOR 4 SERVINGS:

4 large (about 800–900g) all purpose or floury potatoes
about ¼ cup milk
½–1 cup grated cheese
salt and pepper to taste
1 x 440g can filling, e.g. spaghetti, baked beans, chilli
    beans or chilli con carne
relish or sour cream, optional

Scrub the potatoes, then bake or microwave until tender (see Ways to Bake Potatoes, page 32). Cut off the top third lengthwise from each potato and scoop out most of the flesh, leaving a shell. Mash half of the potato flesh with the milk, grated cheese, and salt and pepper. Use the other half at a later date.

Pile the potato mixture into the shells and top each one with a generous amount of canned filling. At this stage you can set aside the prepared potatoes for reheating later.

Reheat the stuffed potatoes in the oven or microwave.

Put the potatoes on an oven tray and bake for about 20–30 minutes at 180°C in a preheated oven until the shells and their filling are hot right through or allow 3–4 minutes per potato at 70% power in a microwave oven. Depending on the canned filling, top each potato with a spoonful of your favourite relish or with a teaspoon of sour cream.

Serve for lunch or as a main meal with a salad or cooked vegetables.

NOTE: Reheated potatoes can be very hot, so take care when you dive in.

Spanish Omelet

This is such an excellent recipe we think you should teach your children and grandchildren how to make it, too! This dish can be found throughout Spain – but with slight variations. So feel free to modify this recipe yourself.

FOR 2 SERVINGS:

3 large waxy or all purpose potatoes (about 600g)
3 Tbsp oil
2 large eggs
½ tsp salt

Scrub and cut the potatoes into cubes.

Heat the oil in a smallish non-stick frypan, then tip in the potatoes. Cover and cook until tender, about 5–10 minutes (the potatoes need not brown).

Beat the eggs and salt with a fork. Tip the cooked potatoes into the beaten egg, then tip the mixture back into the hot pan after adding a dribble of extra oil.

Cook, uncovered, tilting the pan occasionally, until the omelet is nearly set. Slide it from the pan onto a plate, and flip it back into the pan to brown the uncooked side.

Serve the omelet alone, or with salad vegetables.

VARIATIONS: Add a chopped onion to the pan with the potatoes. Mix a chopped red and/or green pepper or chopped cooked vegetables into the potato and uncooked egg mixture.

NOTE: The omelet works best when the mixture almost fills the pan it is made in.

Patata Frittata

A frittata is a cross between an omelet and a crustless quiche. Make it when you want something quick and easy, or when you haven't bought any special ingredients, and want to use up small amounts of various quick-cooking vegetables from your fridge or garden.

FOR 4–6 SERVINGS:

50g butter
3 onions, sliced
3–4 medium (about 450–600g) all purpose potatoes, scrubbed and sliced
2–3 zucchini or other vegetable, sliced
4 eggs, preferably large
2 Tbsp water
½ cup grated parmesan cheese

Melt the butter in a large non-stick frypan or use a heavy iron pan. Cook the onions in the butter over a moderate heat until they are lightly, but evenly browned. Add the potato, stir well, then cover the pan and cook for 15–20 minutes, stirring occasionally. After 10–15 minutes, add the zucchini. Firmly press the vegetable mixture down into the pan.

In a bowl beat the eggs with the water and half the cheese. Pour over the vegetable mixture, jiggling the pan to get rid of any air pockets under the egg mixture, then cook over a gentle heat for 10 minutes or until the sides and bottom have set.

Sprinkle the remaining cheese over the top, then brown the frittata, still in the pan, under a grill until the top is set, nicely puffed and lightly browned.

Leave to stand for a few minutes until the frittata firms up, then carefully cut it into slices taking care not to damage the non-stick surface of the pan. Alternatively, slide the frittata out of the pan onto a large round plate before cutting it.

NOTE: It is not always easy to stop a frittata (or other food) sticking to a heavy iron pan. When cleaning the pan, always get rid of any stuck-on food particles (steel wool is good for this). Rinse the pan well, then rub canola or other oil over the inner surface then heat until it is very hot. When it has cooled down, rub it with a paper towel then coat it with non-stick spray. Finally, rub it gently one more time, again with a paper towel.

Potatoes start off with no fat in them. Chips are enormously popular, but, of course, they have added fat! Chips which are cut so they are thick and chunky, and cooked at a good, high temperature (about 185°C for 3–4 minutes) contain considerably less fat than finely cut (shoe-string) potato chips.

Jane's Potato Flan

Jane, a friend of many years' standing, gave Alison this recipe. She found it to be very popular when it was served for lunch with a salad, as well as being a good addition to a buffet meal.

FOR 3–4 SERVINGS:

400g ready-made flaky pastry
1 cup cottage cheese
1 egg, beaten
¼ cup sour cream
1 tsp salt
2 tsp spring onions, finely chopped
1 cup mashed potato
about 2 Tbsp grated parmesan cheese

Preheat the oven to 220°C.

Roll out the pastry until it is nice and thin and use it to line a 20cm flan tin or pie plate.

Combine the cottage cheese, egg and sour cream in a food processor or blender (press them through a sieve if you want a really smooth mixture).

Add the salt, spring onion and mashed potato and process again until combined.

Turn the potato mixture into the unbaked crust and sprinkle liberally with the cheese. Bake for 30–40 minutes until the pastry and the top are lightly browned.

Serve warm with one or more salads such as cubed tomatoes and marinated green beans.

Hot-smoked Fish and Potato Flan

Alison often makes a fishy variation of Jane's Potato Flan (see above) using a side of hot-smoked, locally caught fish from the fish counter at her local supermarket. She flakes about a cup of flesh, carefully removing all skin and bones. Next, she chops the flesh with a sharp knife and folds it through the flan filling, along with a few dashes of Tabasco or a similar hot pepper sauce before putting the fishy mixture into a 23cm flan tin or pie plate, lined with pastry as in the main recipe, and bakes it at the same temperature, for the same length of time.

Picnic Pie

Celebrate summer! Line a picnic basket with a cheerfully checked teatowel, pack inside it this pie, some fresh fruit and something cold to drink, and set off for a picnic at your favourite beach or park. It's even more enjoyable if you arrange for another family to meet you there. Perhaps they could take something different – such as a rotisseried or roast chicken, bread rolls and tomatoes. It is always more fun when you put the contents of two picnic baskets together! Enjoy!

FOR ABOUT 6 SERVINGS:

400g flaky pastry
3–4 eggs
3 Tbsp milk
2 ham steaks, cubed, or 4–6 slices bacon, cooked and
    chopped
2 sprigs mint, chopped
4 spring onions, finely chopped
4 medium (about 300g) waxy or new potatoes, cooked,
    cooled and cut into cubes
1 cup cold cooked peas or 1½ cups cooked green beans

Preheat the oven to 200°C.

Roll out the pastry on a floured board into two thin rounds or rectangles, reserving scraps to decorate. Set one round aside and use the other to line a 23cm pie plate or a shallow, rectangular baking dish. Trim edges level with the edge of the plate or baking dish.

In a large bowl mix the eggs with the milk to combine whites and yolks. Reserve 1 tablespoonful to use for a glaze.

Add the ham or bacon, mint and spring onion, the potato and the peas or beans. Mix well.

Tip the filling into the pastry-lined plate. Dampen the edges of the second sheet of pastry and place it on top of the filling. Pinch the edges together and fold them under. Press around the edge with a fork if you like. Decorate the top with the pastry scraps and glaze with the reserved egg. Cut a few steam vents in the centre.

Bake for 30 minutes, lowering the heat if the pastry browns too quickly. Cool on a rack and wrap in a teatowel, rather than in plastic or foil, to keep the pastry crisp.

NOTE: You can vary the filling of a pie like this as much as you like except for the number of eggs. They are particularly important because they hold everything together. Although we prefer not to add any salt when bacon or ham is included, and only cook the potatoes in lightly salted water, you may like to add some extra. Don't include any raw ingredients that need long cooking.

Self-crusting Vegetable Quiche

A crustless quiche is a very good addition to any cook's repertoire. It is much easier than making a pastry-based pie, and it looks and tastes good. We serve these quiches for lunch, hoping there will be leftovers for packed lunches the next day. Our favourite quiches contain new (or fairly new) potatoes, and fresh green vegetables such as asparagus, broccoli or tender little green beans. We sometimes add some red pepper or arrange tomato slices on top for extra colour (tomatoes actually in the quiche can make it a bit sloppy). If not over-beaten, this mixture should separate during cooking, forming a firmer layer, or crust, below the well-flavoured filling. You can make it in a loaf tin or a square tin instead of a round one, which is good if you want to cut the quiche into squares or rectangles instead of wedges.

FOR 4–6 SERVINGS:

1 Tbsp butter
1 large onion, chopped
2 cloves garlic, chopped
3 medium (about 300–450g) waxy or all purpose
    potatoes, cooked
3 large eggs
¾ tsp salt
1 cup milk
½ cup self-raising flour

1 cup cooked asparagus, spinach, mushrooms or
    broccoli, well drained and chopped
1 cup grated tasty cheese
1–2 tomatoes, thinly sliced, optional

Position a rack in the middle of the oven and preheat to 220°C.

Melt the butter in a frypan. Cook the onion and garlic in the butter until tender. Cut the potatoes into 1cm cubes. Add to the pan and cook for 1 minute further, then set aside to cool.

Beat the eggs, salt and milk together with a fork. Pour the egg mixture into a large bowl containing the flour, stirring with a fork or whisk until just combined. Add the potato, the drained vegetables and the cheese. Stir gently to mix before pouring into a lightly sprayed or buttered 20–23cm non-stick metal pan or another suitable pan of similar size, but do not use a springform pan with a removable base. Garnish with the tomato if using.

Bake for 20–30 minutes until the quiche is lightly browned and set in the centre. Remove from the oven and leave to stand for at least 5 minutes.

Serve hot, warm or cold, with a tomato or green salad, or cut into small rectangles and serve as finger food.

Cheesy Onion Flan

This tasty flan makes a popular and economical family meal. Leftovers go well in school lunches, too. It is also a useful dish to make if you are cooking for vegetarians.

FOR 4–6 SERVINGS:

50g very cold butter
¾ cup flour
¼ cup grated cheese
2–3 Tbsp cold water
1 Tbsp oil
1 large onion, chopped
1 large clove garlic, chopped
1 tsp cumin
½ tsp oregano
3 large new potatoes (about 300g), cooked and cubed
3 large eggs
¼ cup milk
½ tsp salt
1 cup tasty grated cheddar cheese
pinch of paprika

Using a food processor, chop the butter into the flour. Add the first measure of cheese, then with the motor running add the cold water, drop by drop, until the mixture forms a ball.

Transfer the ball of dough to the lightly floured bench and roll out thinly. Line a 23cm pie plate or flan tin with the resulting pastry and chill until the filling is ready.

Preheat the oven to 220°C.

Heat the oil in a frypan and add the onion and garlic. Cover and cook gently over moderate heat until the onion is transparent and lightly browned. Stir in the seasonings, then the potatoes. Mix well and cook, uncovered, until the potatoes start to sizzle. Remove from the heat.

Break the eggs into a bowl. Add the milk and salt and mix with a fork to blend. Add the potato mixture and stir to mix. Tip the filling into the chilled pie crust.

Sprinkle the surface of the filling with the second measure of cheese and the paprika. Bake for 20 minutes or until the pastry is golden brown and the filling has set.

Cut the flan into pieces for easy serving. It may be eaten cold or reheated, preferably with a salad.

Minted Holiday Pie

Feeding a houseful of hollow-legged children? Carry this pie to the nearest park, beach or playground or, if the weather does not co-operate, into your TV room!

FOR 8–12 SERVINGS:

400g flaky pastry
6 frankfurters
5 medium (about 750g) waxy or all purpose potatoes, cooked
2 cups cooked peas, beans or leeks
1 Tbsp chopped mint
6 eggs
½ tsp salt
4–6 tomatoes, fresh or canned (if using canned tomatoes, ensure they are well drained)

Roll out a little more than half of the pastry until it is very thin. Use it to line a large roasting pan, allowing the pastry to overhang by a few centimetres. Roll out the remaining pastry even more thinly so it is large enough to cover the filling and set aside.

Preheat the oven to 220ºC. Cut the frankfurters into small chunks and slice the potatoes. Spread half the potato, peas and mint and all the chopped frankfurters over the pastry in the pan.

Break the eggs, one at a time, onto a saucer. Using a fork, beat each one enough to break the yolk, then pour it around the chopped frankfurters. Reserve about 1 teaspoon of beaten egg to glaze the pastry top later. Scatter the remaining vegetables evenly over the egg, then sprinkle with salt.

Slice or chop the tomatoes and arrange them evenly over the pie filling.

Spread the second pastry sheet over the filling. Dampen the overhanging edges with water and gently lift them, then press them down over the top. Pinch the edges together and shape attractively if desired. Brush the reserved egg over the surface and pierce the top to make about 12 holes. Bake for 15 minutes or until golden brown, then reduce the heat to 150ºC and bake for a further 15 minutes.

Serve the pie warm or cold, cut in squares, with carrot and celery sticks and bread rolls to fill any gaps.

Neptune's Potato Pie

Alison dreamed up the name of this pie, which combines inexpensive canned smoked fish fillets and potatoes, to make it seem more inviting to her children.

FOR ABOUT 6 SERVINGS:

400g flaky pastry
2 large (about 500g) all purpose potatoes, cooked
1 x 300–425g can smoked fish fillets, drained and flaked
3 large eggs
½ cup chopped spring onions
1 cup grated tasty cheese

Preheat the oven to 200ºC. Roll out the pastry on a floured board into two 23cm circles. Line a pie plate of the same size with one of the circles.

Cut the potatoes into 1cm thick slices and place in a large, shallow mixing bowl. Add the flaked fish, unbeaten eggs, spring onion and grated cheese. Mix carefully, stirring the eggs through the mixture without breaking up the potatoes too much.

Tip the filling into the pie plate. Dampen the surface of the remaining pastry circle with cold water. Place, damp side down, over the pie filling. Press the outer edges of the pastry together, then trim 2cm beyond the pie plate edge. Fold the overhang under the edge of the lower crust and crimp if desired. Cut a vent in the middle of the pie.

Bake for 30–40 minutes or until the pastry has browned evenly and the centre is firm when pressed gently.

Serve wedges cold or warm as part of a summer meal with one or more salads.

 Always handle potatoes carefully – although they may seem tough, they bruise easily if you drop them or treat them roughly, so for best flavour and less waste, look after them!

Cottage Pie

This recipe makes a delicious cottage pie, but with a twist in that it can be cooked in a slow cooker or, if you prefer, it can be baked traditionally in the oven.

This recipe can be doubled but do check that your slow cooker – and the container in which the pie will cook – is large enough.

FOR 2–3 SERVINGS:

600–700g floury or all purpose potatoes
1 onion
1–2 carrots
1 stalk celery
250g minced beef
1 Tbsp flour
1 Tbsp tomato concentrate
1 Tbsp Worcestershire sauce
½ cup stock or 1 tsp instant stock powder dissolved in
     ½ cup water
2 tsp butter
milk as required
¼ cup grated cheese
pinch of ground paprika, optional

(If using your slow cooker, select a heatproof dish that is big enough to hold minced meat for 2–3 servings and which will fit inside.)

Peel and quarter the potatoes. Cook, covered, in lightly salted water until tender.

Finely chop the onion, carrot and celery in a food processor or grate them. Put the prepared raw vegetables and mince into a large non-stick frypan. Brown the mixture, stirring regularly, adding a little oil if necessary to avoid it sticking. Stir in the flour, tomato concentrate, Worcestershire sauce and stock, and bring to the boil. Take the mixture off the heat and spoon it into the non-stick sprayed prepared dish.

Drain the cooked potato and mash with the butter. Beat with a fork, adding enough milk to make a smooth creamy mixture. Spread over the top of the meat and vegetable mixture, swirling the surface attractively. Sprinkle with the grated cheese and add a little paprika for extra colour if desired. (Refrigerate for up to 24 hours at this point).

To cook in a slow cooker: Place the prepared cottage pie in the slow cooker. Add enough cool water to come 1cm up the side of the pie plate. Cover and cook on LOW for 8–10 hours.

To cook conventionally: Place in a preheated 180°C oven and bake for 30–40 minutes.

Serve with a green salad.

Potato Pan Pizza

This useful, quick recipe can be made with some leftover cooked potato (or microwave about 350g potato, but let it cool first) that's great for a quick weekend lunch. Once you are familiar with the recipe, you can make additions and variations of your own.

FOR 2 LARGE OR 4 SMALLER SERVINGS:

1¼–1½ cups cooked all purpose or floury potatoes
1 large egg
1–2 spring onions, chopped
oil for frying
½ cup self-raising flour

TOPPINGS:

½–1 cup grated cheese
1 large or 2 small firm tomatoes
about ¼ cup chopped salami or bacon
sliced black olives, optional

Chop the cooked potatoes, then mash them roughly with a fork.

Using a fork, beat the egg in a bowl and add the spring onion. Add the prepared potato and stir it through the egg mixture.

Put a large frypan on low heat. Just before you are ready to add the flour to the potato dough, raise the heat under the pan to medium heat and brush the surface with a little oil, spreading it evenly over the surface.

Stir the flour into the potato, then shape the mixture into a ball and roll out on a piece of baking paper sprinkled with just enough extra flour to stop the dough sticking until it is the same size as the base of the frypan (the potato dough should be uncracked and even around the outside edge). Discard any flour left on the baking paper and reserve. Slide the pizza base into the hot pan.

Cook the base for 3–4 minutes until the underside is an even golden brown. Slide it out of the pan onto the baking paper, then slip a large plate underneath the pizza. Add a little more oil to the pan and when hot flip the pizza back into the pan, browned side up.

Preheat the grill.

Spread the toppings on top of the pizza while it is still in the pan. When the underside has browned, put the pan under the grill to melt and lightly brown the cheese.

Slide the cooked pizza from the pan onto a rack or serving board. Cut into the required number of portions and eat while warm.

Mushroom & Potato Pie

This single crust pie is simple to make and makes a great winter meal. Its impressive appearance is matched only by its delicious flavour!

FOR 4 SERVINGS:

3–4 medium (about 500g) waxy or all purpose potatoes
1 medium onion
2 Tbsp olive or canola oil
1 tsp minced garlic
200g brown mushrooms
½ tsp dried basil or 1 Tbsp basil pesto
¼ tsp dried thyme
½ tsp salt
black pepper to taste
1 cup sour cream
½ tsp salt
black pepper
1–2 sheets pre-rolled flaky pastry
milk or lightly beaten egg to glaze

Preheat the oven to 220°C.

Scrub the potatoes, then cut into 5mm slices. Place in an oven bag or in a covered microwave dish and cook at 100% power for 10 minutes, stirring gently after 5 minutes.

Alternatively, boil the sliced potato until just tender, handling them gently to avoid breaking them up.

Peel and slice the onion while the oil heats in a large frypan. Add the onion and garlic and sauté until the onion is soft and transparent.

While the onion cooks, slice the mushrooms, then add them to the pan along with the herbs, salt and pepper. Cook, stirring frequently, until the mushrooms have wilted.

Lightly oil or spray with non-stick spray a 20x25cm casserole or deep pie plate. Arrange half the potato slices evenly over the bottom of the dish, then cover with the mushroom mixture and top with the remaining potato slices. Stir together the sour cream and a little extra salt and pepper and spoon over the potato-mushroom mixture in an even layer.

Roll out the pastry (if necessary), until it will cover the casserole/pie plate. Lay the pastry gently over the filling mixture, trimming off any excess. Decorate the edge by patterning it with the tines of a fork and puncture the pastry at 5cm intervals over the surface. Brush with a little milk or beaten egg to glaze, then bake at 220°C for about 15 minutes until the pastry is golden brown.

Serve with a salad or cooked vegetables and some crusty bread.

Curried Sausage & Potato Pie

This recipe has been a favourite in Alison's house for many years. The woman who sent it to her wrote at the time that she had several teenage sons – making it easy for us to imagine them sitting round the table, happily tucking in! We hope their families now enjoy the same recipe just as much as their fathers did!

FOR 4–6 SERVINGS:

5–6 medium (about 1kg) floury or all-purpose potatoes
2 medium onions
1kg sausage meat
1 Tbsp curry powder
2–3 Tbsp brown sugar
1 x 400g can apple sauce or 2 cups cooked and drained apple
pinch of ground cumin, oregano, and salt, optional
1 Tbsp butter
freshly ground black pepper
½ cup milk
½–1 cup grated cheese

Thinly peel the potatoes and cut into even-sized pieces. Cook, covered, in lightly salted water until tender.

While the potatoes are cooking, finely chop the onions.

Next, coat the inside of a small roasting pan or a large, shallow baking dish with non-stick spray. Layer three-quarters of the chopped onion in the bottom of the dish. Working with wet hands, form the sausage meat into sausage shapes and arrange them over the onion. Sprinkle the remaining onion on top.

Preheat the oven to 180°C.

Mix together the curry powder and brown sugar and sprinkle evenly over the sausage and onion layers, then spread over the apple sauce. Sprinkle over the cumin, oregano, and salt if using.

Drain and mash the potatoes with the butter, pepper and milk, then beat with a fork until creamy. Spread over the sausages, swirl or roughen the top attractively, then sprinkle with the grated cheese.

Bake, uncovered, for 1 hour.

Serve as a main meal with several cooked vegetables or a green leafy salad.

Smoked Fish Pie

This useful pie, popular with all age groups at any time of year, is mostly made from store-cupboard ingredients. Adding a vegetable in the sauce with the fish, and a mixed or green salad served alongside the pie adds contrasting colours and textures.

FOR 3–4 SERVINGS:

600g floury or all purpose potatoes, scrubbed
2 large eggs
3 Tbsp butter
3 Tbsp flour
1 cup milk
½ cup liquid from the canned fish (see below) or extra milk
1 x 310g can smoked fish fillets or larger can salmon, drained and flaked
1 can whole kernel corn or mushrooms in brine
½ spring onion, chopped
¼ cup chopped parsley
salt
butter and milk for mashing potatoes
2–3 Tbsp grated cheese
paprika

Choose a heatproof 4 cup capacity baking dish that you can use to serve the pie and which will fit in your slow cooker (if using). Coat the inside of the dish with non-stick spray.

Quarter the unpeeled potatoes lengthwise. Place in a pot with the eggs and cook, covered, in lightly salted water until the eggs are hard-boiled and the potatoes are tender. Drain the potatoes and remove their skins. Cool the cooked eggs in cold water, then peel and chop.

Melt the butter in a pot over moderate heat and stir in the flour. Let the mixture bubble, then add the milk. Stir the sauce until it thickens. Add the extra liquid to the white sauce and stir until it comes to the boil again.

Stir the flaked fish, corn, spring onion, parsley and chopped egg into the sauce. Add salt to taste. Turn the mixture into the prepared heatproof dish.

Mash the potatoes with a little butter and milk. Beat with a fork to a creamy consistency. Spoon onto the fish mixture, swirling the top attractively. Sprinkle with the grated cheese and a little paprika. Refrigerate if not cooking immediately.

To cook in a slow cooker: Place the prepared fish pie in the slow cooker. Add enough water to come 1cm up the side of the pie plate. Cover and cook on LOW for 4–8 hours, taking it out when it suits you.

To cook conventionally: Place in a preheated 180°C oven and bake, uncovered, for 30–40 minutes.

Serve with a green salad or coleslaw.

VARIATIONS: Add a variety of cooked vegetables, e.g. cooked peas, corn, diced carrots, etc, to the sauce.

Potatoes to Die For

Alison's friend Sharon gave her this recipe some years ago and although she always feels a certain degree of guilt as she pours in the sour cream, she justifies it by the fact that she makes it only as an occasional treat.

FOR 4 MAIN COURSE SERVINGS:

10 medium (about 1.5 kg) floury potatoes
3 large cloves garlic
¼ cup flour
½ tsp salt
2 cups low fat sour cream
½ cup milk
200g gruyère cheese

Scrub the potatoes and cut into 5mm slices, dropping them into a large container of cold water as they are prepared. Ensure all the slices are separated, in order to remove the starchy liquid on the cut surfaces. Transfer the drained potatoes to a microwave dish or oven bag, cover the bowl or tie the bag loosely, and cook for about 15 minutes at 100% power in a microwave oven until tender.

Make the sauce while the potatoes cook. Finely chop the garlic, then add it to a medium-sized bowl, mixing until smooth with the flour, salt, sour cream and milk.

Preheat the oven to 180°C.

Butter or spray a 23x30cm ovenproof dish. Make an overlapping layer of half of the potatoes in the dish. Drizzle half the sour cream mixture over, then grate on almost half the cheese. Repeat with the remaining ingredients, then grate the rest of the cheese evenly all over the top.

Bake, uncovered, for about 30 minutes until the mixture feels firm and the topping is golden brown. Remove from the oven and leave to stand in a warm place for 5–10 minutes before serving.

Serve as a main meal with a mixed green salad in a tart, mustardy dressing.

VARIATION: For an extra-special treat, top with 200–300g hot-smoked salmon, broken into flakes and spread over the central part of the browned surface of the potatoes as soon as the pie is removed from the oven.

Oakhill Potatoes

Alison learnt how to make this recipe when she was one of a group of university students, planning, then cooking a pre-ball dinner on a very limited budget. Different members of our family have made it over the years, and it still keeps stealing the show, disappearing before other dishes at many a party over the years! Although it requires some time and effort, you can double or triple the recipe, make it a day in advance, and refrigerate it until needed.

FOR 4–6 SERVINGS:

4 large (about 800g) cooked, all purpose or floury
    potatoes
2 hard-boiled eggs, peeled and roughly chopped
2 rashers bacon
1 medium onion
50g butter
¼ cup flour
1 tsp dry mustard
1 tsp salt
2 cups milk
½ cup grated tasty cheddar cheese
1 Tbsp butter
1 cup fresh breadcrumbs

Slice the cooked potatoes into a shallow, sprayed or buttered baking dish. Add the eggs.

Chop the bacon and onion and cook them together in the first measure of butter in a large pot until the onion is transparent. Stir in the flour, mustard and salt, half of the milk then bring to the boil, stirring constantly. Add the remaining milk and bring to the boil again. Take off the heat and stir in the grated cheese straight away. If the sauce seems too thick to pour easily, thin it with some extra milk. Pour the sauce over the potatoes, covering the entire surface.

Top the sauce with buttered crumbs made by melting the second measure of butter and stirring it into the crumbs.

Refrigerate for up to 24 hours or bake immediately, in the middle of the oven, at 180°C for 30–45 minutes until the potato mixture has heated through and the crumb topping is golden brown.

Serve as part of a buffet dinner or as a family meal, with a salad and small bread rolls.

VARIATION: For a vegetarian meal, leave out the bacon and use twice as much cheese.

Potato, Bean & Bacon One-pan Dinner

This is our version of a dish which is based on a Swiss recipe given to us by our friend, Chris, who has made it regularly for her family over the years. It's wonderful to go out in the garden, just as Chris does, to dig up smallish new potatoes, then to pick young green beans, and be eating the meal just half an hour later.

You can also make it using small white washed potatoes and beans from the supermarket.

FOR 2 SERVINGS:

2 Tbsp oil
1 medium onion
350–400g new or waxy white washed potatoes
200–250g green beans
1 thickly sliced ham steak, about 200g
salt and pepper

Gently heat a large frypan, preferably with a non-stick finish, and with a close-fitting lid. Add the oil and swirl it round so the bottom of the pan is covered.

Chop the onion into small squares and sprinkle the pieces over the bottom of the pan. Cover.

Wash or scrub the potatoes and cut the smallest ones into quarters lengthwise or larger potatoes into 2cm cubes. Arrange them over the onions and replace the lid.

Top and tail the beans and cut them into pieces about 5cm long and arrange over the potatoes.

Cut the ham steak into 1cm cubes and sprinkle them over the beans. Sprinkle a little salt and pepper over, and replace the lid.

Cook over gentle to moderate heat. Any resulting liquid turns to steam and cooks the vegetables in about half an hour. At the end of the cooking time there should be no liquid left.

Serve in two shallow bowls as a complete meal.

VARIATION: The ham steak can be replaced with a similar weight of bacon end, or thickly sliced bacon, either of which should be finely chopped and added to the pan after putting in the oil.

Holiday Hash

We don't think it's necessary to feel apologetic when we cook something like this for a holiday meal.

This is a good one-pan meal, perfect to cook if you're away from your kitchen, on holiday perhaps, and although you don't need to peel the potatoes (see page 4), you do need to precook them.

Alison remembers cooking this mixture in a campground kitchen, impressing the other campers by her foresight in bringing with her in a chilly bin her precooked potatoes. They were also very impressed by the final product!

FOR 4 SERVINGS:

4 large (about 800g) all purpose or floury potatoes, cooked
1–2 cups cubed meat, e.g. corned beef, ham steaks, luncheon sausage, canned Spam, frankfurters or cooked sausages
about ¼ cup chopped gherkins, cucumber or other pickle
4 spring onions, chopped
¼ cup chopped parsley
milk
butter or oil for frying

Roughly chop or mash the cooked potatoes with a fork. Mix with the cubed meat, chopped gherkins, spring onion and parsley. If the potato and meat mixture looks a little dry at this point, add just enough milk to dampen it so it will stay together during cooking.

Heat a 20–23cm non-stick frypan or electric frypan. Add enough butter or oil to coat the base and sides, then add the potato mixture. Cover and cook on a low-to-moderate heat until a crust forms around the bottom and sides (about 20–30 minutes). Carefully run a knife around the edge so it does not stick, then slide out the hash cake onto a plate. Add a little more butter or oil, then slide the hash cake back into the pan again, cooked side up.

To serve, cut into quarters. It is particularly nice served with tomatoes and coleslaw or a lettuce salad.

Fish Cakes

Everyone loves fish cakes. They may not be glamour food, but serve them up and watch them disappear!

FOR 2–4 SERVINGS:

2 cups cold mashed potato
1 large egg
1 cup self-raising flour or scone mix
about 1 cup canned tuna, salmon or smoked fish, drained with liquid reserved
about 2 Tbsp chopped parsley or fresh herb of choice
milk to mix
extra flour
oil for frying

Using a fork or a potato masher, mix the mashed potato and egg with the flour or scone mix. Add the drained fish and the chopped herbs. Mix with a knife or stirrer (see page 96), using some of the reserved liquid from the can and a little milk if necessary, until the mixture is firm enough to shape into cakes. Add extra flour or scone mix if the mixture is too soft.

Using wet hands, form the mixture into 8 cakes, then lightly dredge them in the extra flour.

Heat the oil to a depth of 3–5mm in a heavy-bottomed frypan or electric frypan. When the oil is hot, cook the cakes for 4–5 minutes on each side until they are evenly browned and cooked in the centre. Do not shorten the cooking time or the centres of the fish cakes will be pasty.

Serve with Thai sweet chilli sauce and a salad.

VARIATIONS:

Make without the egg.

Replace the fish with chopped ham etc.

Add chopped spring onions or fresh herbs etc.

 Buy potatoes in big bags to get most for your money! Keep them in a cool, dark place (but not in the refrigerator) in a paper bag or cardboard box – not in a plastic bag.

Thai Green Chicken & Potato Curry

With a little practice, it's possible to make this quick, tasty and popular curry – Thai curry paste is available at most supermarkets – in less than half an hour! Because we especially like the flavour of kaffir lime leaves, we grow the trees from which they come at home, but they are available at Asian food stores and markets and can be frozen for later use. However, if you can't find them, just make the curry without them, or add ordinary lemon or lime leaves.

FOR 4 SERVINGS:

2 Tbsp canola oil
2 Tbsp Thai Green Curry Paste
2 medium onions, quartered then sliced
4 medium (about 450g) new or waxy white washed
　　potatoes, scrubbed and cut into 1.5cm cubes
4 kaffir lime leaves, optional
2 zucchini, sliced
500g boneless and skinless chicken thighs or breasts,
　　cubed
1 x 400ml can regular or light coconut cream
200g green beans, cut into 3cm lengths
2 Tbsp fish sauce
2 tsp sugar
salt to taste
handful of fresh basil leaves, optional

Heat the oil in a large frypan, wok or pot with a lid. Stir in the curry paste and cook for about 2 minutes, then add the onion, potato and lime leaves and stir-fry for 5 minutes.

Stir in the chicken, then add the coconut cream. Cover and simmer for 10 minutes.

Add the prepared vegetables. Cover and simmer for about 10 minutes until the chicken and potatoes are cooked and the vegetables are tender. Add the fish sauce and sugar, with salt to taste, then stir in the basil leaves just before serving.

Layered Lamb & Potato Bake

Simon's wife Sam labelled this as one of the most delicious dishes he has ever turned out of his slow cooker. Not a bad compliment, considering how easy it is to make. It's so good we've given conventional cooking instructions too, for those who don't yet have a slow cooker.

FOR 6 SERVINGS:

800g all purpose or floury potatoes
½ tsp salt
1 large onion
1 large clove garlic
1 Tbsp oil
1.2–1.5kg (about 8) lamb shoulder chops
1 x 400g can diced tomatoes in juice
2 Tbsp tomato paste
1 Tbsp balsamic vinegar
1 tsp dried oreganum
salt and pepper
chopped basil or parsley to serve, optional

Turn a medium-to-large slow cooker to LOW and coat with non-stick spray. (If baking conventionally, non-stick spray a 3-litre casserole dish.) Peel and thinly slice the potatoes. Arrange the potatoes in a layer in the slow cooker or casserole dish and sprinkle with the salt.

Peel and chop the onion and garlic. Heat the oil in a medium frypan, add the onion and garlic and cook until the onion has softened.

While the onion cooks, arrange the lamb chops in a layer on top of the potatoes.

When the onion is ready, stir the tomatoes and juice, tomato paste, vinegar, and oreganum into the pan. Season to taste, then bring the sauce to the boil.

Pour the onion and tomato mixture over the lamb.

To cook in a slow cooker: Cover and cook on LOW for 8–10 hours.

To cook conventionally: Cover the casserole dish with a close-fitting lid or sheet of foil, then bake in a preheated oven for 2–2½ hours at 150°C or until the lamb chops are almost falling off the bone.

To serve, carefully move the chops to one side. Divide the potatoes between plates, place a chop on top of each and spoon over some of the sauce. Garnish with a little chopped basil or parsley if desired.

Peppery Chickpea & Potato Curry

The spiciness in this simple curry comes largely from black pepper, which gives an interesting heat that is quite different from chilli. We make it using a fairly mild curry powder, which gives flavour but does not mask the pepper effect.

FOR 3 SERVINGS:

1 tsp black peppercorns
2 large cloves garlic, peeled
2–3 Tbsp chopped coriander leaves
1 Tbsp canola oil
1 Tbsp mild curry powder
2 medium (300–500g) waxy or new potatoes, scrubbed and diced
1 x 400g can chickpeas, rinsed and drained
2 medium tomatoes, diced
¾ cup coconut cream
½ cup hot water
1 Tbsp soy sauce
½ tsp sugar
salt to taste
1–2 Tbsp chopped coriander leaves, extra

Measure the peppercorns into a blender or mortar and pestle. Add the garlic and the coriander leaves and blend or pound to a paste. Add the oil and mix well.

Transfer the paste to a medium large non-stick frypan and cook over a medium heat, stirring frequently, for 2–3 minutes or until fragrant. Stir in the curry powder and cook for a further 1–2 minutes.

Add the prepared potatoes, chickpeas and tomatoes. Stir to coat with the spice mixture, then add the coconut cream, hot water, soy sauce and sugar. Bring to the boil, then reduce the heat to a gentle simmer and cook, stirring frequently, for 10–15 minutes or until the potato cubes are cooked through.

Season to taste with salt, garnish with the chopped coriander and serve. A cucumber salad and some naan bread make great accompaniments.

NOTE: If preferred, replace the coconut cream with ¾ cup light and creamy evaporated milk plus ¼ tsp coconut essence.

Scalloped Potatoes with Tuna

Scalloped potato mixtures are always popular. Using a packet soup mix creates a particularly flavourful mixture, and adding tuna turns it into a substantial meal. This recipe works remarkably well in a slow cooker but we've given instructions for either baking or slow cooking.

FOR 4 SERVINGS:

1kg floury or all purpose potatoes, scrubbed
2 medium onions, diced
1 x 220g can tuna, drained and flaked
250g sour cream
½ cup milk
37g packet onion or bacon and onion soup mix
1 cup grated cheese
pinch of paprika to dust

Cut the scrubbed potatoes into 2–3mm thick slices.

Thoroughly coat the bowl of the slow cooker or a shallow casserole dish with non-stick spray. Sprinkle half the diced onion into the bowl. Cover with half the sliced potatoes, then crumble over the tuna. Sprinkle in the remaining onion and arrange the rest of the potato in another layer on top.

Combine the sour cream, milk and soup mix in a small bowl. Pour evenly over the layered potato mixture, then sprinkle the top with the grated cheese and dust lightly with paprika.

To cook in a slow cooker: Set the slow cooker to HIGH and cook for 4–5 hours.

To cook conventionally: Preheat the oven to 220°C. Cover the casserole dish (use the lid or a sheet of foil folded loosely over the edges) and bake for 30 minutes. Uncover and bake for a further 30 minutes until the cheesy topping is evenly golden brown and the potatoes in the centre are tender.

VARIATION: Make without the tuna and serve as a side dish for 6 people.

 Did you know that potatoes have been given the Heart Foundation's tick of approval? For heart health, watch that you don't add too much fat or salt to your potatoes.

Vegetarian Shepherd's Pie

This recipe must be one of the most popular recipes in our book Meals Without Meat. So many people tell us that everyone in their family really enjoys it, often without realising that it contains beans rather than meat!

FOR 4–6 SERVINGS:

6 large (about 1kg) all purpose or floury potatoes
2 Tbsp butter
1 cup grated cheese
milk
2 large onions, roughly chopped
2 Tbsp butter
1 red or green pepper, deseeded and chopped
3 Tbsp flour
1 tsp instant vegetable stock powder
1 tsp each basil, oregano, paprika and soya sauce
1½ cups water, beer, wine, bean liquid and/or the potato cooking liquid.
2 Tbsp tomato concentrate
1 x 440g can red kidney beans, drained

Thinly peel the potatoes, then cut into chunks. Simmer in lightly salted water until tender. Drain, reserving the cooking liquid.

Mash the potatoes with the first measure of butter, half the grated cheese, and enough milk to make a fairly soft consistency. After mashing, beat the potatoes with a fork until they are light and fluffy.

In a large pot cook the onions in the second measure of butter until they are tender and well browned. Add the pepper and flour and stir until the flour is lightly browned. Add the remaining ingredients except the beans, then bring to the boil, stirring constantly. Add the beans, either whole or roughly chopped or mashed. Taste and adjust the seasoning as required.

Spread the bean mixture into a lightly sprayed 20x25cm baking dish. Cover with spoonfuls of the mashed potato, spreading it to cover the beans. Sprinkle the remaining grated cheese over the surface.

Cook, uncovered, at 180ºC for 20–30 minutes or in a microwave oven (about 5 minutes on High, 100% power) until the bottom centre feels hot. Brown the top under a grill after microwaving, if necessary.

VARIATIONS: For a traditional Shepherd's Pie, replace the beans with about 2 cups of roughly chopped cold roast lamb or hogget.

Irish Stew

Although it is not traditional, we like to precook the onion and garlic for this stew. A mixture of fresh herbs, as well as the traditional parsley, gives it a very good flavour. Like others in this chapter, we originally developed this version for a slow cooker, but it can be cooked as a casserole.

FOR 3–4 SERVINGS:

2 tsp oil
2 large onions, cut into 1cm cubes
1 large clove garlic, chopped
500g all purpose or floury potatoes scrubbed
¼ cup chopped fresh herbs (parsley, sage, thyme etc.)
about 600g trimmed lamb shoulder meat, cubed
1 tsp salt
½ tsp pepper
¼ cup flour
1 tsp balsamic vinegar
½ cup chicken stock or ½ cup water and ½ tsp instant stock powder
extra chopped fresh parsley to garnish
cornflour mixed with a little water to make a paste, optional

Thoroughly coat the bowl of the slow cooker or a large casserole dish with non-stick spray. Turn the slow cooker on to HIGH or preheat the oven to 160°C.

Heat the oil in a non-stick frypan with a lid. Add the onion and garlic and cook for about 5 minutes, stirring occasionally.

Cut the potatoes into 2cm cubes. Put half the onion in the bottom of the prepared slow cooker or casserole dish. Layer half the potato cubes on top, and sprinkle with half the chopped herbs. Repeat the layers using the rest of the onion, potato and herbs.

Toss the cubed lamb with the salt, pepper and flour, then place the lamb on top of the vegetables. Pour over the vinegar and stock.

To cook in a slow cooker: Cover and cook on HIGH for 5–7 hours. After 4 hours, gently fold the meat through the vegetables. This should be nicely cooked after 5 hours, but the meat becomes even more tender on longer cooking.

To cook conventionally: Tightly cover the casserole dish, then place in the oven and cook for 2½–3 hours, stirring the stew gently after about 2 hours.

Add the cornflour paste to the liquid to thicken if desired.

Serve, generously sprinkled with the chopped parsley, with green beans or broccoli, and carrots.

NOTE: Although it is not traditional, you can add cubed carrots to this stew.

Pizza Potatoes

Because most children love the flavour of pizza, you can use the same combination of flavours here producing a stuffed potato that can be served as the main part of a meal. Most of the ingredients are optional – the only really vital one is the cheese!

FOR 1–2 SERVINGS:

1 large (about 200g) evenly shaped floury potato
1 cup grated cheese
2 spring onions, chopped
1 rasher bacon, chopped and sautéed
¼ cup chopped, sautéed mushrooms or red peppers
¼ tsp dried oregano
1 Tbsp tomato paste
yoghurt, milk, mayonnaise or sour cream to thin
extra bacon and/or chopped olives or anchovies to garnish, optional

Scrub, oil, then bake the potato either in a preheated 200°C oven for 1–1½ hours or at 100% power for 5–6 minutes in a microwave oven, turning it once during the cooking time. Allow 3–4 minutes' standing time after microwaving. Check if it is cooked through by pressing it gently, if cooked the potato should give a little.

While the potato cooks, mix together in a bowl the cheese, spring onion, bacon, mushroom or red pepper, and oregano. Add the tomato paste.

When the potato is cooked, allow it to cool enough to handle then cut in half lengthwise and scoop out the flesh with a spoon. Mash the flesh with the remaining ingredients. Add a little yoghurt or other dairy product if the mixture is dry.

Pile the filling into the potato halves and garnish as desired.

Reheat in a preheated 180°C oven for 15–20 minutes or microwave for 3–4 minutes at 100% power.

Serve alone or with a salad.

 The way potatoes are stored and cooked can affect their nutritional content. To retain most nutrients, prepare potatoes just before you are going to cook them. Don't leave them standing in water or exposed to the air for longer than you have to.

Bacon, Potato and Prune Cake

Based on a Swiss alpine recipe, this unusual filling and delicious main course can be made in a large slow cooker or in a large pot with some space to spare.

FOR 6 SERVINGS:

enough strips of shoulder bacon to line the bowl
2 large onions, sliced into lengthwise slivers
3 cloves garlic, crushed and chopped
2 tsp olive oil
2 large eggs
¾ cup crème fraiche or plain cream plus 2 Tbsp lemon juice
250g pitted prunes
1kg all purpose or floury potatoes

If you are making this in a slow cooker, turn it to HIGH. Choose a 7-cup capacity heatproof bowl that will fit in the slow cooker and coat the inside with non-stick spray.

Line the bottom and sides of the bowl with the bacon, leaving enough hanging over the sides to fold over the filling.

In a frypan, gently cook the onion and garlic in the oil for about 5 minutes.

Mix the eggs and crème fraiche in a separate large bowl. Chop the prunes into pea-size pieces, then add, along with the sautéed onion and garlic, to the egg mixture.

Scrub, then grate the potatoes. Tip into a clean teatowel and squeeze out most of the liquid. Stir the grated potato through the egg mixture, then press into the bacon-lined bowl and fold the ends of the bacon over the top. Cover with foil.

To cook in a slow cooker: Lower the bowl into the slow cooker (use long strips of folded foil as 'lifters'). Add enough warm water to come halfway up the bowl. Cook on HIGH for 4–5 hours or on LOW for 8 hours, checking the water level occasionally.

To cook conventionally: Place the foil-covered bowl in a large pot, adding enough warm water to come halfway up the bowl. Cover the pot and cook for 3–4 hours, checking the water level occasionally to make sure the pot does not boil dry.

When cooked, carefully remove from the slow cooker or large pot and take off the foil lid. Turn out onto a rack as you would a cake. Using a serrated knife, cut into 6 wedges and serve immediately with several lightly cooked vegetables or an interesting leafy salad, depending on the season.

Slow Cooker 'Lazy Daisy' One-pot Dinner

We all have days when we feel exhausted, when something easy and basic for dinner is called for. This fast, easy 'everything in one bowl' dinner will, we hope, make your day easier so you can put your feet up a little sooner. We originally wrote this recipe with slow cookers in mind, but you can cook it in the oven if desired.

FOR 4 SERVINGS:

about 600g chuck steak
2 bay leaves
1 rounded tsp Marmite or other similar spread or 1 Tbsp instant beef stock powder
½ cup boiling water
2 Tbsp balsamic or red wine vinegar
1 medium onion, cut into 1cm cubes
2 large carrots, chopped into 2cm cubes
1 cup sliced celery, optional
4 medium waxy or new potatoes (about 600g), scrubbed and cut into 2cm cubes
2 cups frozen peas
brown sugar and salt to taste
arrowroot, potato starch or cornflour to thicken

Coat the inside of the bowl of a medium-to-large slow cooker with non-stick spray.

Cut the steak into 2cm cubes and add to the slow cooker along with the bay leaves.

In a bowl or measuring jug dissolve the Marmite or instant beef stock in the boiling water and stir well. Add the vinegar, stir again, then drizzle it over the meat. Add the vegetables except the frozen peas.

Cover and cook on LOW for about 8 hours or until everything is tender. About half an hour before serving, turn the slow cooker to HIGH. Put the frozen peas in a large sieve over the sink and run boiling water over them to heat them up. Add them to the cooker and stir. There will be considerably more liquid than you started off with.

Taste the liquid, and add about 1 tablespoon of brown sugar and up to 1 teaspoon of salt to round off the flavour as desired. Then thicken with 1–2 tablespoons of arrowroot or other starch paste mixed with a little water. Cook for a few more minutes until the gravy thickens, then serve in bowls.

VARIATION: Proceed as above, but put everything in a large casserole dish instead of a slow cooker. Bake at 150°C for 1½–2 hours until the meat is very tender.

Murphy's Potato Moussaka

A moussaka is a baked, layered meat and vegetable mixture. Its ingredients vary from country to country, but we love this version with a cheesy, eggy mixture baked on top of layers of tomato-flavoured mince and potatoes. Alison has always found it to be wonderful family food, especially enjoyed by teenagers. Although not traditional, we make it with sliced cooked potatoes and sometimes we'll use a can of tomatoes already flavoured with Italian-style herbs, rather than plain canned tomatoes. The choice is yours.

FOR 6 SERVINGS:

500g mince
2 large onions, finely chopped
2 Tbsp oil
½ tsp salt
2 Tbsp flour
1 x 440g can Italian seasoned tomatoes
5 large (750–800g) all purpose potatoes, peeled and
    cooked

SAUCE:

2 Tbsp butter
2 Tbsp flour
½ tsp freshly grated nutmeg
1 cup milk
1 cup grated cheese
1 egg, beaten

In a large frypan over high heat brown the mince and onion in the oil, stirring frequently. Stir in the salt and flour and cook for 1–2 minutes before stirring in the tomatoes. Continue cooking, stirring, until the mixture boils and thickens.

Cut the cooked potatoes lengthwise into 5mm thick slices. Set aside.

Make the sauce next. Melt the butter, add the flour and nutmeg and cook briefly, stirring constantly. Add half the milk and stir continuously until the sauce thickens. Add the rest of the milk and continue to stir until the sauce boils and thickens. After it boils, take it off the heat and stir in the grated cheese and the egg.

Preheat the oven to 180°C.

Spray or butter a 10–12 cup capacity shallow ovenproof dish and spread with one-third of the potato. Cover with half the mince, one-third of the potato, then the rest of the mince. Top with the remaining potato. Press down the top layer of potatoes to flatten. Pour the cheese sauce evenly over the top layer of potato and bake, uncovered, for about 30 minutes.

Remove from the oven and leave to stand for a few minutes before serving as the main meal of the day with a cooked green vegetable or a green salad.

Sherrean's Bacon, Bean & Potato Savoury

Sherrean, a Californian friend of Alison's, has made this recipe for 50 years. Her daughters, now adults with children of their own, also make it because everyone always enjoys it so much! When Alison makes it using fresh produce from her garden, she's worked out that if she moves fast, she can dig the potatoes while the bacon browns, then pick the beans while the potatoes are starting to cook!

FOR 1 SERVING:

2–3 rashers bacon, rind removed and cut into 2cm long strips
1 small onion, chopped
1 tsp butter
2–3 medium (about 300g) waxy or new potatoes, scrubbed
about 2 Tbsp water
½ tsp chicken or green herb instant stock powder or ¼ tsp salt
oregano and ground cumin to taste
about 100g young scarlet runners or green beans of choice, cut into 5cm lengths
about 1 tsp cornflour mixed to a paste with a little water

Cook the bacon strips in a pan until crisp. Remove and set aside most of it to use as a garnish later on. Add to the remaining bacon and bacon drippings in the pan the onion and butter. Cook until the onion is transparent and just beginning to brown.

Cut the potatoes into quarters and add to the pan along with the water, stock powder or salt and herbs. Simmer for about 10 minutes until the potatoes are almost tender.

Add the beans and cook for a further 10 minutes. If necessary, add a little extra water during the cooking time with the aim of finishing up with about 2 tablespoons of liquid. Thicken the liquid with just enough cornflour paste to coat and glaze the vegetables. Taste and adjust the seasonings if necessary.

Serve in a shallow bowl, sprinkled with the reserved cooked bacon with a tomato salad alongside if you like.

NOTE: Multiply the ingredients to suit the number of people for whom you are cooking.

Potatoes Plus

Most of the recipes in this section are favourites of ours, where potatoes cook happily alongside the meat we are cooking for dinner. As well, there is one of our favourite vegetarian curries, and last but not least, delicious home-made fish and chips, made easy! We hope that you will enjoy all of these as much as we do, and that they make your life a little easier!

Chickpea, Spinach & Potato Curry

This makes a great vegetarian meal, easy and delicious on its own, but even more interesting when served with an array of Indian condiments.

FOR 4 LARGE SERVINGS:

2 Tbsp canola oil
1 large onion, diced
2 cloves garlic, crushed, peeled and chopped
1 Tbsp finely chopped root ginger
2–3 medium (about 300g) waxy potatoes, cut into 1cm cubes
2–3 tsp curry powder (mild or hot to taste)
½–1 tsp cumin seeds, optional
2–3 bay leaves
1 x 250g package frozen spinach, thawed
1 x 400g can whole tomatoes in juice
1 x 310g can chickpeas, drained
¼–½ cup water, if required
2 tsp garam masala
salt and pepper to taste
2 Tbsp chopped fresh coriander

Heat the oil in a large pot. Add the onion, garlic and ginger and stir-fry until the onion has softened and is turning clear. Add the potatoes, curry powder, cumin seeds if using, and the bay leaves. Cook for 1–2 minutes then add the spinach with its liquid and the tomatoes in juice. Crush the tomatoes, then stir in the chickpeas.

Gently simmer for 15 minutes or until the potato cubes are tender, adding a little water if the mixture begins to look too dry. When the potatoes are cooked, add the garam masala and season to taste with salt and pepper. Add the chopped coriander.

For a simple meal serve in bowls as is. Alternatively serve with rice, naan bread or poppadums and assorted chutneys and relishes.

Slow Cooked Glazed 'Roast' Lamb with Potatoes

Alison thinks that this reasonably priced and rectangularly shaped small forequarter lamb roast with some rib bones on its underside is one of the nicest and easiest meat dishes she has ever cooked in her slow cooker. Its coating makes a very attractive and tasty glaze as the meat cooks, while the bones are easy to remove when the meat is cooked to the well-done stage, resulting in boneless meat that can be carved into slices from top to bottom.

FOR 24 SERVINGS:

700–1100g lamb forequarter roast
1–2 Tbsp dark soy sauce
1–2 Tbsp Wattie's Asian Chilli Sauce
1 tsp sesame oil
4–8 small (about 500g) waxy or washed white potatoes
2 large carrots or other root vegetables, cut in large chunks
2–3 tsp cornflour
½–¾ cup boiling water

Coat the inside of the bowl of a medium-to-large slow cooker with non-stick spray and turn to LOW.

Locate the top part of the front leg bone (or the shoulder blade), so you know where to find it when it's time to remove it after cooking.

Mix together the dark soy sauce, chilli sauce and sesame oil. Rub the mixture all over the meat, then place in the slow cooker, rib-side down.

Rub the vegetables with any remaining coating and arrange around the meat. Cover and cook for 7–8 hours, by which time the meat should have an attractive brown glaze.

Lift out the cooked meat and place on a board. Lift away the rib bones first then, using a knife, remove the bone surrounded by meat. Slice the meat and set aside to keep warm while you make the gravy.

Lift out the vegetables and set aside while you make the gravy. Stir the cornflour into the dark pan drippings, then stir in the boiling water. Don't forget to turn off the slow cooker after this step.

Serve the sliced lamb with the roasted vegetables and gravy, and with green peas or another green vegetable of your choice.

VARIATION: To cook conventionally, roast the lamb shoulder in a roasting pan, loosely covered with a tent of tin foil. Cook at 160°C for 2–3 hours, or according to individual preference.

Easy Beef Pot Roast with Potatoes

This excellent pot roast is very easy to make because you don't need to brown anything first. You will need to ask your butcher to tie the meat into a neat roll because you are unlikely to find chuck steak rolled and tied at the supermarket – or even in most New Zealand butcher shops. Alison's helpful butcher says that the shoulder end of the chuck makes a more tender pot roast than the neck end.

FOR 6 SERVINGS:

1.5–2kg chuck steak, about 12cm x 18cm, tied
dark soy sauce
2 tsp garlic salt
½ tsp oregano
½ tsp ground cumin
½ tsp paprika, preferably smoked
6–8 medium (about 700g) waxy or new white washed potatoes
2 stalks celery, cut into 5cm lengths
3 large carrots, each cut into thirds
2 large onions, quartered
1 x 400g can tomatoes in juice
salt and pepper
½ tsp sugar
1 cup beef stock (if cooking in the oven)

Coat the inside of the bowl of a medium-to-large slow cooker (or a large casserole dish with a close-fitting lid) with non-stick spray. Turn the slow cooker to LOW (or preheat the oven to 130°C–140°C).

Pat the meat dry with a paper towel and rub it all over with the soy sauce. Combine the next four ingredients in a bowl and mix thoroughly. Sprinkle over the top of the meat and then transfer to the slow cooker or casserole dish.

Arrange the prepared vegetables round the meat. Add the tomatoes and juice.

To cook in a slow cooker: Cover and cook on LOW for 8 hours. At the end of this time, turn the cooker to HIGH. Lift out the cooked meat and vegetables and set aside to keep warm while you thicken the liquid in the cooker with arrowroot or potato starch mixed to a paste with a little cold water. Season to taste, including the sugar.

To cook conventionally: Add the stock to the casserole dish, then cover tightly. Bake for 3–4 hours or until the meat is tender, checking once or twice during this time to ensure there is always some liquid in the casserole dish.

Slice the meat and serve with the slow-cooked vegetables, the thickened gravy and a briefly cooked green vegetable.

NOTE: The size and weight of a rolled chuck roast should not make a difference to its cooking time.

Pork & Paprika Casserole

Alison created this easy casserole many years ago when Simon was a baby and Kirsten was not much older. Alison remembers waiting for the butcher to cube the shoulder pork for her, while Kirsten would be busy investigating everything within reach.

If the paprika in your store cupboard is stale and brown rather than red, throw it out and buy a fresh lot.

FOR 4 SERVINGS:

2 tsp canola or olive oil
2 medium onions, chopped
2 cloves garlic, chopped
600g lean shoulder pork, cubed
200g button mushrooms, halved
1 red pepper, deseeded and chopped, optional
1 cup sliced celery, optional
1 Tbsp paprika
1 Tbsp instant chicken stock powder
½ cup water or white wine
4–6 medium all purpose or floury potatoes
cornflour, arrowroot or potato starch to thicken
chopped parsley leaves to garnish

To cook in a slow cooker: Heat the oil in a frypan. Add the onion and garlic and cook over low to moderate heat until the onion is lightly browned and has turned clear.

Cut the cubed pork into smaller pieces if desired, then tip into the slow cooker. Add the mushrooms, and the pepper and celery if using, and then the onion mixture. Sprinkle the paprika and instant stock over the bowl and toss the contents to mix. Add the water.

Scrub or peel the potatoes, then halve them and arrange round the inside of the slow cooker, with the cut surfaces closest to the edge. Cover and cook on LOW for about 8 hours or on HIGH for about 4 hours. A few minutes before you turn off the cooker, thicken the liquid with some cornflour, arrowroot or potato starch paste (made by adding a little water), stirring it in gently.

To cook conventionally: Preheat the oven to 180°C. Heat the oil in a large casserole dish. Add the onion and garlic and cook over low to moderate heat until the onion is lightly browned and turned clear. Add the remaining ingredients and stir gently, then cover tightly and bake for 1½ –2 hours.

Sprinkle with chopped parsley just before serving alongside a quickly cooked green vegetable or a green salad.

Malay Beef & Potato Curry

Although this curry requires long slow cooking, the actual 'hands on' preparation time is quite short. Don't be put off by the long list of ingredients, either. They are mostly spices, which are added in two batches. If you don't have all of them on hand, just leave them out – with the exception of the five-spice it will make little difference in the end.

FOR 4–6 SERVINGS:

1kg gravy beef
2 Tbsp ground coriander
1 Tbsp ground cumin
2 tsp five-spice powder
1 tsp each chilli powder, turmeric and ground cinnamon
½ tsp ground cloves
3 Tbsp canola oil
1 medium onion, quartered and sliced
4 cardamom pods, crushed
2.5-5cm piece cinnamon stick
1 whole star anise star
6 cloves
2 cups water
1 x 400g can coconut cream
4 medium (about 600–700g) all purpose potatoes, cubed
1–1½ cups fresh or frozen green beans, optional
2–3 Tbsp lemon juice
1–2 tsp salt

Trim any obvious fat from the meat, then cut into cubes. Place the meat in a medium sized bowl. Measure in the first seven spices and toss to coat.

Heat the oil in a large heavy pot or casserole dish. Add the onion, cardamom, cinnamon stick, star anise and cloves and cook over moderate heat until the onion is soft and golden brown.

Add the spice-coated meat to the pot and cook, stirring frequently, for about 10 minutes. Stir in the water, increase the heat and bring the contents of the pot to the boil. Reduce the heat to a gentle simmer, cover, and cook, stirring occasionally, for 1 hour.

Pour in the coconut cream and add the potatoes. Stir well, cover and cook for a further 45–60 minutes, or until the beef is very tender. Add the beans if using, lemon juice and salt to taste. Simmer, uncovered, for 5 or so minutes until the beans are tender.

Serve on its own or over steamed rice, accompanied with Malaysian roti (bread).

Pork Sausages, Peppers & Potatoes

When we make this easy and really delicious recipe, we always use red, orange and yellow peppers, rather than green ones which can give the mixture a slightly bitter flavour. Their colour after slow cooking is also less than attractive.

FOR 4 SERVINGS:

8 good quality pure pork sausages
2 large onions
4 cloves garlic
4 plump, crisp peppers, preferably 2 red, 1 orange and 1 yellow
½ tsp salt
freshly ground pepper to taste
½ tsp dried thyme leaves
½–1 cup chicken stock or white wine
4 largish all purpose or floury potatoes
cornflour, potato starch or arrowroot to thicken, optional

To cook in a slow cooker: Coat the inside of the bowl of a medium slow cooker with non-stick spray. Evenly brown the sausages in a non-stick frypan over moderate heat, turning them often and pricking in a number of places to stop them bursting.

Cut the onions in half from top to bottom, and remove the skins. Cut the onion halves into lengthwise slivers and transfer to the slow cooker. Peel and chop the garlic and add to the onion.

Cut the peppers in half from top to bottom. Remove and discard the stems, seeds and membranes, then cut into long thin slices. Add to the onion and garlic in the slow cooker.

Sprinkle with the salt, pepper and thyme, then place the browned sausages on top and drizzle with ½ cup of stock.

Wash, thinly peel and quarter the potatoes. Place around the sausages, ensuring the cut surfaces touch the sides of the slow cooker.

Cover, turn to HIGH and cook for 4 hours or LOW for 7–8 hours. When the sausages are cooked, thicken the liquid if desired with some paste made from a little cornflour, potato starch or arrowroot mixed with cold water. It is easier to stir this evenly through the liquid if you remove the potatoes and sausages first.

To cook conventionally: Preheat the oven to 180°C. Put the prepared onions, garlic and potatoes in a large well-sprayed or oiled casserole dish with a tight-fitting lid. Top with the sliced peppers, then sprinkle with the flavourings and stock. Add all the stock, then arrange the browned sausages on top.

Cover the casserole dish tightly, putting a piece of tin foil under the lid if you think it is necessary to stop the liquid evaporating while it is in the oven. Cook for 1¼–1½ hours or until the potatoes are tender. Thicken any remaining liquid with a little cornflour paste just before serving.

Serve with a green side salad.

Lynley's 'Gingered Up' Corned Beef Dinner

It is always nice when a friend shares a recipe with you, especially one that's not only novel and easy to make, but also tastes very good!

FOR 6–8 SERVINGS:

1.5kg piece corned silverside, preferably evenly shaped
1.5 litres ginger ale (about ⅔ of a large bottle)
½ orange
1 cinnamon stick
4–6 cloves
2–3 cloves garlic, optional
6–8 medium waxy or new potatoes, peeled or scrubbed

Rinse the corned beef, then place in the slow cooker or a pot with a tight-fitting lid. Add enough ginger ale to half-cover the meat. If you have no other use for the remaining ginger ale, you can use the whole bottle without affecting the recipe.

Cut the orange into several slices and add to the beef, along with the cinnamon stick, broken into several pieces, and the cloves. Peel the garlic if using, then thoroughly squash each clove with a flat-bottomed glass bottle, then add them to the cooker or pot. Place the potatoes, whole or chopped according to your preference, around the corned beef.

To cook in a slow cooker: Cover and cook on LOW for about 8 hours.

To cook conventionally: Place the covered pot on the stove and bring to the boil over moderate heat, then simmer gently for about 2½ hours.

Sauce: Melt 25g of butter in a pot with 1 tablespoon of canola or other oil. Stir in 3 slightly rounded tablespoons of flour, then add, ½ a cup at a time, 1½ cups of the corned beef cooking liquid, stirring or whisking as you go, and bringing to the boil after each addition. To turn this into a mustard sauce, simply stir in 1 rounded teaspoon of Dijon or other mustard of your choice. It's even more delicious if you also add 1 tablespoon of cream or sour cream before bringing the sauce back to the boil.

To serve, mash the potatoes or leave whole. Slice the meat and serve hot with vegetables of your choice.

Roast Beef with Potatoes

Roasts don't get much simpler than this one, which requires just 10–15 minutes' preparation. Then you've just got to put it in the oven and come back in an hour.

FOR 4–6 SERVINGS:

1.2–1.5kg beef topside roast
2 cloves garlic, peeled and sliced
2 Tbsp Dijon mustard
1 Tbsp olive oil
1 Tbsp dark soy sauce
1–2 tsp fresh or dried thyme, optional
1–2 tsp fresh or dried rosemary, chopped, optional
1–1.2kg all purpose or floury potatoes, scrubbed
1 teaspoon instant chicken stock powder
1 cup boiling water
2 cloves garlic
2 Tbsp olive oil
salt and pepper to taste

Pierce the beef at intervals with a sharp knife and insert a sliver of garlic into each cut. Measure the mustard, oil, soy sauce and herbs, if using, into a large plastic bag. Massage the bag to mix the contents, then add the beef. Massage the bag again so the paste covers the entire roast. Leave to stand for at least 15 minutes but longer if possible (up to 24 hours if refrigerated).

Preheat the oven to 180°C.

Cut the potatoes into 1–1.5cm thick slices, then arrange them so they overlap in the bottom of a small roasting pan or shallow casserole dish. Add the stock powder to the boiling water and pour into the pan. Peel, crush and chop the garlic and add to the pan with the olive oil and salt and pepper to taste.

Place the meat on a wire rack and position it over the potatoes in the pan. Cook for 1–1¼ hours, depending on how well done you like your beef. (A meat thermometer is useful for checking doneness – the temperature at the thickest part should be 50°C for rare or 60°C for medium).

Stand the cooked beef in a warm place for 10–15 minutes before carving, collecting any juices to add to the gravy (see Note below).

Serve on warmed plates with gravy and one or more lightly cooked seasonal vegetables.

NOTE: To make a tangy gravy, combine and heat 1–2 tablespoons Dijon mustard (smooth or whole grain), ½ cup red wine and ½ cup other liquid (e.g. vegetable cooking liquid or stock) and any juices collected during resting or carving.

Lemon-Garlic Roasted Chicken & Vegetables

Roast chicken dinners are special for all sorts of reasons. This version is a favourite for two reasons: it tastes great and it's really easy!

FOR 4–6 SERVINGS:

1 chicken, about 1.5–1.8kg
1 large or 2 small lemons
3–4 cloves garlic
2–3 sprigs each fresh thyme and tarragon (or rosemary)
1–2 Tbsp olive oil
salt and pepper
1–1.5kg roasting vegetables, e.g. floury potatoes, kumara, parsnip, pumpkin, red/green/yellow peppers etc.
2–3 Tbsp olive oil
1–2 cloves garlic, extra
3–4 sprigs fresh thyme and tarragon or rosemary, optional

GRAVY

2 Tbsp flour
2 Tbsp olive oil
1–1½ cups chicken juices, stock, water or white wine
salt and pepper to taste

Preheat the oven to 200°C.

Rinse the chicken inside and out, removing any giblets etc. Pat dry. Pierce the lemon/s about six times with a sharp knife, then crush and peel the first quantity of garlic. Place the lemon and garlic inside the chicken along with the fresh herbs.

Place the chicken, breast side up, in a large roasting bag and add the olive oil. Massage the bag so the whole chicken is coated with the oil, then tie the bag leaving a finger-sized gap at the opening for the steam to escape. Place the bag in a large roasting pan and transfer to the oven to start cooking while you prepare the vegetables.

Scrub or peel the root vegetables, depending on your preference, then halve or quarter them lengthwise depending on their size. Cut the pumpkin into 4–5cm chunks and deseed and quarter the peppers. Crush, peel and chop the second quantity of garlic. Place all the prepared vegetables in a large unpunctured plastic bag, add the oil and toss to coat.

Remove the vegetables from the bag and arrange them, except the peppers, in the pan around the bagged chicken. Add the peppers 20–30 minutes later as they require less time to roast.

After about 1¼ –1½ hours, carefully remove the roasting pan from the oven. If the vegetables have not browned sufficiently, place them under the grill for a few minutes.

Snip a corner of the oven bag and collect any juices to make gravy (see below), then slit open the whole bag with a sharp knife and pierce the thickest part of the thigh with a sharp knife to check if the chicken is cooked, in which case the juices should run clear, not pink.

Carve or break up the chicken as required and arrange the meat and vegetables on a warmed platter or serving plates.

Measure the flour and oil into a non-stick frypan and mix to a smooth paste. Cook over a high heat until the mixture begins to colour, then gradually add the liquid and stir continuously to prevent lumps forming until the gravy boils and thickens. Season to taste.

Spray oils are fantastic for potatoes – you add much less oil but still get the wonderful crispy, crunchy result!

The water in which potatoes are cooked has a surprising amount of flavour. Use it, alone, or mixed with other vegetable cooking liquid, as liquid for gravy or to replace some of the milk in white or cheese sauce, or add it to stocks and soups.

Potatoes have so much flavour and nutrients in, or just under their skins, so it's a pity to throw it away. Try rubbing washed potatoes with "green scratchies" otherwise known as rectangular green plastic pot scrubs. These take off the dirt, leave most of the skin intact – and you finish up with more potato for your money.

If you MUST peel potatoes, use a sharp potato peeler in preference to a vegetable knife. The peeler removes a thinner layer than the knife does – so you save money too!

Oven-baked Fish & Chips

If your family likes fried fish and chips, but you don't like the last-minute work involved, try "oven frying" both the fish and the chips. As well as producing good results, it uses only a small amount of oil.

FOR 4 SERVINGS:

4 large (about 800g) all purpose or floury potatoes
1 Tbsp oil
4 boneless, skinless fish fillets (150g each)
½ cup self-raising flour
½ tsp salt
½ tsp sugar
½ tsp ground cumin (optional)
½ tsp dried oregano (optional)
½ tsp paprika (optional)
2 Tbsp oil
1 or 2 eggs

Turn the oven to 230°C with two shelves, one a little below the middle, the other above the first, near the top of the oven.

Scrub the potatoes and cut them lengthways first into halves, then into quarters, and then into eighths. Dry with a tea towel or paper towels. Put in a large plastic bag and drizzle with the first measure of oil. Shake gently, to lightly coat with the oil.

Place prepared potatoes in a large, shallow baking dish lined with baking paper and bake on the lower shelf for about 30 minutes, turning chips once or twice. Use the fan if your oven has this option.

While the chips cook, prepare the fish fillets. Mix the flour with the seasonings in a shallow bowl. Line another shallow metal dish, big enough to hold the fish in one layer, with baking paper and coat with non-stick spray. Beat the egg with a fork, just enough to combine the white and the yolk evenly.

When the chips are nearly cooked (about 12 minutes before you want to eat), put the prepared baking dish in the oven to heat for about 1 minute. While it heats, pat the fillets dry and coat first with the seasoned flour, then with the beaten egg, then again with the flour. Working fast, put the fillets in the preheated, sprayed dish and drizzle the remaining oil over them.

Cook the fish on the shelf above the chips for about 8 minutes altogether, turning with a fish slice after 5 minutes. Take the fish from oven as soon as the centre of each fillet seems cooked (it will be dry and tough if overcooked).

Serve the fish and chips promptly, with lemon or lime wedges and a side salad.

Growing your own potatoes

If you have the space, it is very satisfying to plant a few rows of potatoes in your back garden, watch them grow into healthy plants, and eventually to dig them up and find for each potato you planted you now have a dozen new healthy ones. We have always found that children or grandchildren enjoy helping with the harvest too!

Growing times

Depending on how long they take to grow, varieties are divided into early, early main and main crop. Choose varieties that suit your preferred time of harvest. (See below for a selection of varieties.) It's a good idea to experiment with new varieties to find the ones which best suit your growing conditions and taste preferences.

Height / spread

Potato plants grow about 50cm tall. Each plant can spread 80–90cm, depending on the variety.

Frost hardiness

Potato plants are not frost hardy but will usually re-sprout after a frost.

Sun, soil, water, food

Potatoes of all types grow best in open soils in a sunny, well-drained position. They also grow well in sandy soil if plenty of well decayed compost and manure has been mixed in before planting, and if they are watered regularly. Blood and bone or a balanced fertiliser also helps get good results.

Potatoes suitable for growing in the NZ home garden

EARLY POTATOES – these usually have a waxy texture, and are suitable for boiling and salads.

Early potatoes include:

Swift — Round, white skin and cream flesh. Very early.

Rocket — Round-oval, white skin and flesh.

Cliff's Kidney — An old, kidney shaped variety known for good quality.

Jersey Benne — Another old kidney shaped variety with good quality.

Liseta — oval, light yellow fleshed tubers.

EARLY MAIN CROP POTATOES – Most of these can be dug while the leaves are growing and bushy, or they can be left for longer until the plants become more mature and the leaves collapse and die.

Maris Anchor — Round-oval white fleshed tubers. Can be dug early or left to mature.

Ilam Hardy — Round-oval white skin and flesh. Vigorous grower which can be dug early or left until mature. They have a floury texture when mature.

Karaka — Round-oval white skin and flesh. Tendency to develop growth cracks in uneven growing conditions but exceptional flavour and are all-purpose potatoes.

Potatoes are usually grown, not from seeds, but from small "seed potatoes". Those suitable for planting should be 50–100g in weight with small sprouts starting to appear on them. Plant seed potatoes 5cm deep and 25–30cm apart, in rows 50–80cm apart. This makes the process of 'earthing up' easier (see below).

Care/maintenance

When the plants are 20cm high build up the soil ('earth up') around the plants, covering some of the new shoots and lower leaves but leaving about 10cm uncovered. Continue the process at two weekly intervals until the plants flower. Earthing up protects plants from late frost, warms the soil and helps retain moisture. It also prevents the tubers from turning green when they are exposed to light, thereby ensuring a better crop.

Growing potatoes in pots and tubs

Potatoes can be successfully grown in pots and tubs with drainage holes. Fill a large bucket with 10–15cm of free draining soil or potting mix and add a generous handful of a fertiliser containing a NPK of 5 / 7 / 4. Place a seed potato on top of this mix and cover it with soil. As the potato emerges add more soil mix every second week just leaving the top of the plant exposed until the bucket is full. Allow the plant to mature and flower. Simply tip out the potato plant and the soil to get the potatoes!

Harvesting potatoes

Potatoes can be harvested early while the tops are still green. At this stage, the tubers will be immature and small, but their flavour will justify the lower yields at this stage. Grow early maturing varieties for early harvest.

Pests and diseases

Those new to potato growing should ask the staff at garden centres for advice. Virus diseases are less likely if certified seed potatoes, produced especially for planting potatoes, are used.

Purple Passion — This is a new release, with purple skin and light yellow flesh. Exceptional flavour and texture when dug while tops are still green.

Nadine — Attractive round tubers with white skin and flesh. Sets high number of tubers which need regular watering to size up. Waxy texture but lacks flavour.

Katahdin or Chippewa — An old variety, round with white skin and flesh. Mainly suited to boiling.

Driver — Round tubers with white skin and flesh. Vigorous grower. Good for boiling and salads.

Heather — Oval tubers with purple skin and white flesh. Suitable for most end uses and can be left to mature.

MAIN CROP POTATOES — These are best when grown to full maturity. Suitable for storage.

Moonlight — Now the most popular variety in New Zealand. Oval with white skin and flesh. Easy to grow with high yield of good tasting tubers suitable for boiling and frying.

Agria — A popular variety with oval tubers and yellow flesh. Suitable for most purposes.

New potato varieties, with new names, are always being developed. Do not expect to see all the varieties mentioned here on sale. Some varieties do better in a particular part of the country, so will not be available everywhere.

Index

Knives etc., by Mail Order

For about 20 years Alison has imported her favourite, very sharp kitchen knives from Switzerland. They keep their edges well, are easy to sharpen, a pleasure to use, and make excellent gifts.

VEGETABLE KNIFE $8.00
Ideal for cutting and peeling vegetables, these knives have a straight edged 85mm blade and black (dishwasher-proof) nylon handle. Each knife comes in an individual plastic sheath.

BONING/UTILITY KNIFE $9.50
Excellent for boning chicken and other meats, and/or for general kitchen duties. Featuring a 103mm blade that curves to a point and a dishwasher-proof, black nylon handle. Each knife comes in a plastic sheath.

SERRATED KNIFE $9.50
These knives are unbelievably useful. They are perfect for cutting cooked meats, ripe fruit and vegetables, and slicing bread and baking. Treated carefully, these blades stay sharp for years. The serrated 110mm blade is rounded at the end with a black (dishwasher-proof) nylon handle and each knife comes in an individual plastic sheath.

THREE-PIECE SET $22.00
This three-piece set includes a vegetable knife, a serrated knife (as described above) and a right-handed potato peeler with a matching black handle, presented in a white plastic wallet.

GIFT BOXED KNIFE SET $44.00
This set contains five knives plus a matching right-handed potato peeler. There is a straight bladed vegetable knife and a serrated knife (as above), as well as a handy 85mm serrated blade vegetable knife, a small (85mm) utility knife with a pointed tip and a smaller (85mm) serrated knife. These elegantly presented sets make ideal gifts.

SERRATED CARVING KNIFE $28.50
This fabulous knife cuts beautifully and is a pleasure to use; it's ideal for carving or cutting fresh bread. The 21cm serrated blade does not require sharpening. Once again the knife has a black moulded, dishwasher safe handle and comes in a plastic sheath.

COOK'S KNIFE $35.00
An excellent all-purpose kitchen knife. With a well balanced 19cm wedge-shaped blade and a contoured black nylon handle, these knives make short work of slicing and chopping, and have come out on top of their class in several comparative tests. Each dishwasher-safe knife comes with its own plastic sheath.

VICTORNOX MULTIPURPOSE KITCHEN SHEARS $29.50
Every kitchen should have a pair of these! With their comfortable nylon handles and sharp blades these quality shears make short work of everything from cutting a piece of string or sheet of paper to jointing a whole chicken. Note: Black handle only.

STEEL $20.00
These steels have a 20cm 'blade' and measure 33cm in total. With its matching black handle the steel is an ideal companion for your own knives, or as a gift. Alison gets excellent results using these steels. N.B. Not for use with serrated knives.

PROBUS SPREADER/SCRAPER $7.50
After her knives, these are the most used tools in Alison's kitchen! With a comfortable plastic handle, metal shank and flexible plastic blade (suitable for use on non-stick surfaces), these are excellent for mixing muffin batters, stirring and scraping bowls, spreading icings, turning pikelets etc., etc…

NON-STICK LINERS
Re-usable SureBrand PTFE non-stick liners are another essential kitchen item – they really help avoid the frustration of stuck-on baking, roasting or frying. Once you've used them, you'll wonder how you did without!

Round tin liner	(for 15-23cm tins)	$6.50
	(for 23-30cm tins)	$9.50
Square tin liner	(for 15-23cm tins)	$6.50
	(for 23-30cm tins)	$9.50
Ring tin liner	(for 23cm tins)	$6.95
Baking sheet liner	(33x44cm)	$13.95
Barbeque Liner	(Heavy duty 33x44cm)	$17.95
Frypan Liner	(Heavy duty round 30cm)	$10.95

All prices include GST. Prices current at time of publishing, subject to change without notice. Please add $5.00 post & packing to any order (any number of items).

Make cheques payable to Alison Holst Mail Orders and post to:

Alison Holst Mail Orders
FREEPOST 124807
PO Box 17016
Wellington

Or visit us at www.holst.co.nz